T0318173

The Disseminated Self

The *Disseminated Self: Ecosystem Perspective and Metapsychology* explores attitudes to climate change and ecological disaster from a psychoanalytic perspective.

The author examines the concept of Self, how this can be broad enough to encompass our world as well as just our own bodies and why in some cases this still does not allow us to recognize and act on the threat to the self of climate disaster. Drawing on the work of Freud and Winnicott and examining the place of destructiveness in psychoanalysis and in everyday life, this books offers a fresh perspective on the climate change debate. This book broadens psychoanalytic thinking in order to address both individual and societal issues facing the ecosystem disaster. It also develops a complementary psychoanalytic perspective in considering the psychotherapeutic process, with emphasis on the mobilizing and integrative effects of topic translations in mental functioning. Finally, it explores heuristic perspectives for multidisciplinary, comprehensive approaches to human phenomena.

Translated into English for the first time, *The Disseminated Self* uniquely draws on the French psychoanalytic traditions and will be of great interest to the English-speaking psychoanalytic world, as well as any with an interest in climate change and the relationship between Man and the environment.

Jean-Paul Matot is a child psychiatrist, member of the Belgian Society of Psychoanalysis and International Psychoanalytic Association, Director of the Belgian Review of Psychoanalysis and honorary lecturer at the Free University Brussels.

The Disseminated Self

Ecosystem Perspective
and Metapsychology

Jean-Paul Matot

Translated by Anne Burton

Routledge
Taylor & Francis Group

LONDON AND NEW YORK

First published in English 2021
by Routledge
2 Park Square, Milton Park, Abingdon, Oxon OX14 4RN

and by Routledge
52 Vanderbilt Avenue, New York, NY 10017

Routledge is an imprint of the Taylor & Francis Group, an informa business

Translated by Anne Burton

British Library Cataloguing-in-Publication Data
A catalogue record for this book is available from the British Library

Library of Congress Cataloging-in-Publication Data
Names: Matot, Jean-Paul, author. | Burton, Anne (Translator), translator.
Title: The disseminated self : ecosystem perspective and metapsychology /
  Jean-Paul Matot ; translated by Anne Burton.
Other titles: Soi-disséminé. English.
Description: Abingdon, Oxon ; New York, NY : Routledge, 2021. |
  Translation of: Le soi-disséminé : une perspective écosystémique et
  métapsychologique. | Includes bibliographical references and index.
Identifiers: LCCN 2020038158 (print) | LCCN 2020038159 (ebook) |
  ISBN 9780367694029 (hardback) | ISBN 9780367694005 (paperback) |
  ISBN 9781003141648 (ebook)
Subjects: LCSH: Self. | Psychoanalysis. | Human beings—Effect of
  environment on. | Climatic changes—Psychological aspects.
Classification: LCC BF697 .M377 2021 (print) | LCC BF697 (ebook) |
  DDC 155.9/15—dc23
LC record available at https://lccn.loc.gov/2020038158
LC ebook record available at https://lccn.loc.gov/2020038159

ISBN: 978-0-367-69402-9 (hbk)
ISBN: 978-1-003-14164-8 (ebk)

Typeset in Times New Roman
by Apex CoVantage, LLC

Contents

Preface

Michael Parsons

This book seeks deliberately to engage psychoanalysis with the economic and environmental issues facing humanity: an unusual, refreshing and, one could say, a necessary project.

Alongside his clinical and metapsychological works, Freud himself wrote a lot about society and its organization: *Totem and Taboo* (1913), *Civilization and its Discontents* (1930), *Moses and Monotheism* (1939) and more. These texts met with a mixed response from specialists in their fields, and psychoanalysis has always had a somewhat ambivalent relationship to social and political thinking. From early on, however, there have been analysts who do believe there is a necessary connection.

In the 1920s and 1930s, a group that included Otto Fenichel, Wilhelm Reich, Erich Fromm, Siegfried Bernfeld and others thought psychoanalysis should adopt an explicitly left-wing political agenda. The radical nature of psychoanalytic ideas seemed to them to entail a corresponding social and political radicalism. The group scattered when they left Germany after Hitler came to power. Fenichel circulated a series of letters, the *Rundbriefe*, trying to keep their aspirations alive, but the idea of a socially and politically committed psychoanalysis faded away. Emigré analysts felt precarious enough in their new countries without wanting to be seen as troublemakers, and the events of the 1930s had already confirmed the majority of analysts in thinking that psychoanalysis needed to stay well clear of politics (Jacoby, 1983). In 1983, a group was founded in the British Psychoanalytical Society called "Psychoanalysts for the Prevention of Nuclear War". There was predictable disagreement in the Society between those who thought it was essential to take part in combating the nuclear threat and those who thought psychoanalysis, as a profession, should not involve itself in political issues.

It is not always possible to stay out of politics. Authoritarian regimes cannot tolerate a discipline based on values of freedom and autonomy, and under dictatorships, psychoanalysts have been drawn inevitably into political engagement. More positively, analysts contribute actively nowadays to discussion of issues like feminism, racism and the climate crisis.

There is a tension, then, for analysts. Are their social and political views, of whatever sort, just personal opinions with no connection to their psychoanalytic awareness of the internal world? Or does that concern with the internal world necessarily entail a concern with the external issues that face humanity?

In this book, Jean-Paul Matot is unequivocal: psychoanalysts do have to be engaged with those external issues – specifically, in his view, with environmental, ecological and economic issues. This is not a question of morality. According to Matot, analysts are obliged, like it or not, to address these questions because of the essential nature of psychoanalysis.

In psychoanalytic terms, the subject/object relationship is generally seen as a relation based on difference, between a subject and an object that are separate from each other: the symbiotic relationship of early infancy has to be superseded. Matot rejects an ontology based on this kind of binary distinction. The risk, for him, is that a world-view which accepts the usual division between subject and object may disconnect humanity psychologically from the environment it lives in, an environment, Matot would say, that it not only lives in but is part of. For him, it is vital to see humanity and its environment not as separate entities but as a single ecosystem.

Matot's aim is to offer a metapsychology that will accommodate this way of viewing the world. Ego-functions, for example, he prefers to see as functions of an ego-environment system. Boundaries remain important but not in a way that is too rigid or sharp edged. There exist, rather, various kinds of "psychic envelopes" offering different levels of "containment" in the human/environmental ecosystem. The set of functions that regulates human life can thus be seen as unfolding in and out of our bodily envelope. Some functions are purely internal, others are purely external and a whole series of others are both internal and external. Among these, some are supported by a differentiation between inner and outer, while for others, that is less relevant.

The self, as conceptualized by Matot, encompasses the ego but extends more broadly through the entire space, not limited by the bodily envelope, in which the variety of different human functions operates. This leads to the idea of a plurality of psychic envelopes which operate to stabilize psychic functioning. To describe the self, envisioned in this way, Matot introduces the term "Disseminated Self". This is his fundamental concept, and it provides the title of his book.

In his challenge to the distinction between a purely internal and purely external realm, Matot co-opts Winnicott's concept of an intermediate space. The idea of a plurality of envelopes is linked to Bion's concept of "container-contained". Such connections to British and American psychoanalysis – Hans Loewald is another point of contact – along with citations of French analysts and anthropologists mostly unfamiliar in Britain – will be interesting for anglophone readers.

Matot intends, with his concept of the Disseminated Self, to show that psychoanalysis must, of necessity, take as its frame of reference the entire human/environmental ecosystem, in all its variety and complexity. This makes the question of social and political engagement unavoidable. A psychoanalytic book this may be, but its psychoanalytic theory carries a powerful political message. Matot declares that the destruction currently being visited on our planetary environment is due to an attack on the relationship between the Disseminated Self and the ecosystem that it is part of. The worldwide hegemony, he says, of a particular kind of financial ideology relegates the diversity and intricacy of this ecosystem "to a status of exotic curiosity" (p. 20). He writes of the imperialism of the values of this ideology and the "omnipresence of its norms":

> absolute primacy of capital gains over stability of the ecosystem; monopolistic appropriation of techniques that accelerate the reduction of human beings to their market value by the double effect of consumerist "ideals" and managerial violence; the destruction of human beings with their environment by the pervasiveness of hyper-capitalist culture.
>
> (p. 20)

Matot calls this process "a soft genocide" (p. 20). This is strong language. Matot affirms in this book that psychoanalysis can make a unique contribution to understanding the environmental and ecological crises of our time. But such a deliberately provocative phrase goes further. It underlines Matot's insistence not just that psychoanalysis "can" contribute but that it is bound by its nature to be actively engaged and involved in that debate.

I commented earlier that Matot does not frame his argument in terms of a moral obligation for analysts; his point is that they are involved regardless, simply by the fact of being analysts. What this book does imply, however, is that the essence of psychoanalysis makes it a profoundly ethical discipline.

Preface to the French edition

Bernard Golse

Thank you to Jean-Paul Matot for allowing me to write the preface to his new book, but above all, thanks to him for writing it.

I have known Jean-Paul Matot well for many years because he is very committed to the European Association for Child and Adolescent Psychopathology (AEPEA), which I have chaired since 2014 and in which he now occupies an essential role at the level of our association board. So, I know his commitment to psychopathology, especially for its psychoanalytic component.

This text by Matot seems essential and innovative to me. Essential in the face of the incessant attacks on psychoanalysis (and on psychoanalysis in the context of autism in particular), which hardly mask an attack against psychic care in general as well as an attack against the human sciences as a whole, which is also disastrous! But also innovative for the following reason. Many current psychoanalytic writings more often have an identity reassurance function for practitioners left insecure by the attacks mentioned previously than they have a function of a true conceptual creativity. It is a pity, but it is, however, what we can see.

Matot, in contrast, offers us authentic new lines of thought for a living psychoanalysis in the 21st century, something it truly seems to me that we need terribly.

If we could talk, in the past, of a schizophrenic (functioning, in the words of D.W. Winnicott, as a "collection of isolated persons") or depressed society, today, to look closely at what is happening, one might wonder if the functioning of our societies has not instead been gradually organized in a borderline mode. . . .

By this, I mean that psychopathology is in great difficulty at the moment insofar as, in the field of childhood, but not only there, mental disorders are now considered either in purely neurodevelopmental terms (not to say neurological!) or in terms of simple consequences of external, current or more or less recent trauma.

Under these conditions, everything then happens as if there were no longer any room for psychic reality or the internal world and therefore for psychopathology, whose central objective is precisely to understand mental suffering by closely linking the role of internal factors (biological and in particular genetic) and external factors (the effects of encounters with the environment) specific to the development and biography of each subject.

This is the very essence of borderline or limit functioning, which insists on splitting the endogenous from the exogenous and which tirelessly tries to reduce the psychic space and the work of internal elaboration to their congruent portions.

However, not everything can be reduced to the question of neurodevelopmental disorders and post-traumatic stress disorder!

I therefore attach the greatest importance to the concept of "Disseminated Self" that Matot offers us today, because it is not only a concept that requestions the ontological paradigms of psychoanalysis, it is also a concept that has the force of proposition on the metapsychological level and which aims to consider the subject as a fully fledged component of its global ecological system.

Apart from his well-known work on adolescence – *L'enjeu adolescent: deconstruction, enchantement et appropriation d'un monde à soi* (2014) – it seems to me that this new book continues the reflection started by Matot in some of his previous publications (in French): *La construction du sentiment d'exister* (2008), *La psychanalyse: une remise en jeu* (2010) and *L'Homme décontenancé. De l'urgence d'étendre la psychanalyse* (2019).

It seems to me that there is, at the same time in this conceptual trajectory, the desire to open psychoanalysis to the taking into account of the environment in its broadest sense and to propose a new metapsychology which can take account of this opening.

The central idea seems to me, in fact, to be that of a conception of humanity that cannot be dissociated from its environment, which obliges us not to focus too narrowly and restrictively on the traditional subject/object entity.

In the first part of the work, Matot very early recalls the position of Descola (an anthropologist holding the chair of "anthropology of nature" at the Collège de France), according to whom this separation of subject/object is a constitutive fact of what one can designate a "naturalist ontology".

From there, Matot seeks first to re-examine the ontological paradigms of psychoanalysis, and the metapsychological propositions which result from it are the subject of the second part of the work.

While the ecosystem disaster has become glaring (at the time of writing, the Covid-19 epidemic is in full swing!), Matot usefully reminds us that some authors had been warning us for a long time, like Harold Searles, but that psychoanalysts had not wanted to hear them and/or take them into account.

Man is part of a whole, and our angle of vision should not be too narrow, hence the concept of the Disseminated Self as the anchor of reflection on the plurality of envelopes and of praise of non-differentiation carrying transformative potentials such as, perhaps, so-called pluripotent stem cells?

Matot's considerations lead him quite naturally, in this first part, to revisit the issues of destructiveness, omnipotence and the psychosomatic dimension.

Let there be no mistake: reading this first part is not melancholic, even if it is specifically called "environmental melancholy", and by contrast, it seems rather stimulating and invigorating!

As for the second part, it is no more and no less than an invitation to rethink metapsychology in terms of a Disseminated Self beyond the focused structure of the subject and the object.

It is not at all a dilution in a Great Whole which would refer to the "oceanic feeling" as conceived by Ferenczi when he thinks of the fetus but rather a diffraction of the Self beyond the simple body envelope.

This evokes de M'Uzan's already ancient work on "the extra-territoriality of the I" but by extending it beyond the solely interpersonal register.

Then, we may think of a theory of an enlarged Self and no longer of a restricted Self, a little bit as Laplanche proposed it for seduction, like Einstein's approach to relativity (from a theory of restricted relativity to a theory of generalized relativity).

This expansion of the Self beyond our bodily and psychic limits clearly shows that it is not an intrapsychic instance, like the Ego, but rather a particular vision of the links between the Ego and the world around it and to which it belongs.

The notion of "Disseminated Self" is thus opposed to any localization of the mind, and Matot bases this on the assertion by Jean-Claude Ameisen: "The very idea of function is inseparable from the notion of context" (Ameisen J.-C., 1999, p. 251).

From there, Matot's reflection almost inevitably focuses on links as inbetween or interface, whether transitional spaces or networks of transitional phenomena, and he is thus in search of a metapsychological renewal, pleading for a metapsychology which is no longer trapped in the boundaries of the usual subject/object couple.

And this is where I would like to make my modest contribution to this very energizing and dynamic reflection.

If, for a long time, on a methodological level, biologists and neuroscientists have tended to consider the brain in itself, that is to say, out of relation and in isolation, a little like other organs, we recently witnessed the birth of a kind of "relationship biology" (Vincent), as evidenced by a number of biological works in the field of imitation or attachment, for example.

As a result, biologists and neuroscientists globally operated the same movement – *mutatis mutandis* – as that psychoanalysts had carried out when they went from the theory of the drives (in its most endogenous version) to the theory of object relations (in its most exogenous version), a change of perspective which should not, however, be too schematized or radicalized.

All this means that psychoanalysts and neuroscientists find themselves today on the common ground of links, with the success that we know of the concept of intersubjectivity.

This point brings me to the question of object representation, which I naturally consider from my place as a clinician psychoanalyst for very young children.

What exactly is meant by object representation?

Recently, I proposed the idea that the representation of an object gains from being deployed, diffracted and dismantled into three distinct levels: the representation of the place of the object, the representation of links with the object and the representation of the object as such, it being understood that the representation of the place of the object is first (perhaps innate?) and that the representation of links conditions, precedes and prepares the representation of the object, which is later in the course of early development.

The representation of the place of the object refers to the preconceptions of Bion and to the register of the "virtual" as studied today by authors like Missonnier, and on this subject, it is interesting to recall what Darian Leader teaches us in his book on art, namely that there were never more visitors to the Louvre than between 1911 and 1913, a period during which one display was only the empty place left by the *Mona Lisa*, which had been . . . the object of a theft!

This shows the highly mobilizing importance of the place of the object.

As for the representations of the links with the object, it can be said that they far precede the establishment of the representation of the object, which opens onto a metapsychology of the link and perhaps the advent of a third topic very necessary to think about psychoanalysis with babies and with autistic patients, for example.

This third topic, already explored in various fields by authors like Brusset, Dejours and Kaës, can only be a topic of links and their intrapsychic representations.

This topic of links makes it possible to better represent the requests of patients who have little or no differentiation (babies and autistic people, for example) and who cannot therefore address a request (manifest or latent) to a specific object.

In a way, it would be an intransitive, not object-addressed, request, a request translating a movement towards the outside specific to any living organism which oscillates permanently and in a dialectical way between an advance towards the outside and a possibility of withdrawal.

It is there, in my sense, that the dynamics inherent to the Disseminated Self fundamentally linked to its surroundings and in a reflexive quest for the representation of its links with that beyond itself are found.

We can hardly emerge from reading this work without thinking about the observation window that we choose for our theoretical and clinical modelling.

Thanks again to Jean-Paul Matot for helping us to become aware of the fact that without this questioning, it is not only metapsychology which risks drying out, retreating into a niche limited to the anatomical borders of the subject and the object and finally disappearing, but it is also an opportunity that would be missed to question our links with the whole world around us.

This world, if it wants to avoid damaging sociopolitical disasters – and if there is still time – now needs to be thought of using psychoanalysis, but by a living psychoanalysis open to changes in its lenses and iris, to conclude here with a photographic vocabulary.

Bernard Golse is Child Psychiatrist and Psychoanalyst (Psychoanalytic Association of France), Head of Child Psychiatry at Necker-Enfants Malades Hospital (Paris) and Professor Emeritus of Child and Adolescent Psychiatry at René Descartes University (Paris 5).

Foreword
A Cycladic dream

It's hot, even overnight, during this Cycladic summer. I spend the warmest hours of the days working on this book. Some nights, it has even agitated my sleep and entered my dreams.

As dawn approaches, after the swirling winds which have struggled to settle in the north, under the beneficial dominance of the *meltemi* – if it moderates its ardour – I remain stuck in such a dream without being able to wake up.

I am invited to give a lecture in the hospital where, as a medical student, I did my first internships in psychiatry more than 40 years ago; everything has changed, the pavilions from that period have given way to imposing rooms, empty, as high as modern cathedrals.

I park my car on the campus, near where the conference will take place. When I get there, I realize that it is not strictly speaking a lecture hall but rather a kind of very large building, with terraces above on several levels. There are people there who have come to listen to me; I can hear the sound of conversations, without seeing anyone: it seems that all these people are on the terraces, but too far away for me to distinguish them. I wonder if the acoustics are good enough for them to hear me, but I do not dwell on it, focusing on what I am going to talk about. The organizers told me that the theme of the event is prison experience. I have very little experience on the subject; the only time I entered a jail was when I went to see one of my incarcerated patients who was in a poor state. So, I decided to talk about drug addicts, which was accepted. I do not really know what connection I had established between the two, except that some addicts I had met in my career had had several stints in prison. I decided to talk very simply about my clinical experience with addicted patients. So, there I am speaking; the audience seems to be listening to me, although noises of conversations continue to reach me. I then notice that groups of people seem to be moving, walking away, from one terrace to another, from one room to another. I try to join the movement, to keep in touch with the different groups of students who seem to be dispersed in different places of what seems to me more and more like one of these futuristic cities in comic books, except that I still do not see anyone. However, I am aware of the fact that I am moving farther and farther away from the place where I parked my car, asking myself with some anxiety how I am going to find it in this monumental journey my discursive itinerary is taking me on.

Furthermore, the conference ends, because it is time, although I do not have the feeling that I've really reached the end of what I am talking about. This does not seem to bother anyone, so, me either. We are in front of a suburban construction built in the style that I had known in the past. The organizers and the participants scatter in small groups, parked cars start to move away, and I recognize several colleagues with whom I had dealt, without much pleasure, during my career, including the Head of Department of the Academic Hospital, who drives away in a futuristic luxury car that looks like the Batmobile.

I realize that it has probably been planned that I have lunch with them, but as no one has invited me explicitly, I say to myself that if, in addition, they take me to a distant restaurant, I will have even more trouble finding my car, which obviously is not here, and even less time to find it. So here I am, trying to retrace along the random path followed during my presentation, but quickly realizing that I do not recognize any of the places through which I pass, under the impression of going astray more and more. Finally, I reach an area overlooking train and motorway tunnels, which makes me think of a suburb of a large city.

I notice that one of the lanes is occupied by a line of multicoloured vehicles that I date back to the sixties Californian Beatnik period. I then climb a long staircase and find myself in a rather lively square, at a junction of darker alleys that seem ill famed, along which are groups of slouched young men and women looking aimless. I ask a young woman who is waiting in the square to help me find my way, which she seems incapable of doing, despite her good will, not knowing herself where she is or where she is going to, but not appearing to be at all worried about it. I realize that it may take me a very long time to find my car and that I may end up having to give up. Rejecting this possibility, I go into one of the alleys at random, attentive, however, to evaluate possible aggressive inclinations from the scattered human aggregates. . . .I continue my wandering, increasingly discouraged as to my chances of finding the car with which I came . . . while telling myself that I might as well wake up, because obviously I'm wasting my time . . . but holding back, however, at the idea that, if I leave this scene in the dream, I will definitively lose any chance of finding the place where I left my car . . . this lasts quite a time, without anything happening, at least that I can remember. . . .

Yet I woke up, at least I think I did . . . but I really do not know where I could have left my car! Fortunately, it is still parked here, in front of the house . . . it belonged to my mother, who died almost 18 years ago, and is ending its life on a Greek island . . . but was it really this car, in my dream . . . did I know?

Forgive me, reader, for still hoping you will continue reading the following.

Milos, July 2019

Introduction
Reexamining the ontological paradigms of psychoanalysis

Strong and sustained mobilization to fight the suicidal apathy of humankind faced with the destruction of our ecosystems, especially in Western societies, entails in-depth examination of what made it possible.

Psychoanalysis, which throughout the 20th century has enriched Western thought with new understandings of man's ways of acting, thinking and being, should be able to make significant contributions to such a debate that, obviously, must involve all fields of knowledge.

In a recent book, the Swiss psychoanalyst Luc Magnenat (2019) addresses the issue by focusing on two lines of thought based on the work of the British psychoanalyst Wilfred R. Bion (1897–1979):

1   the display of the destruction of the ecosystem may constitute projection spaces of zones of "disaster", related to the avatars, more or less important according to the individuals, of the building of the personality of every human being through interplay with the mothering environment. The defences against this overwhelming anxiety would be akin to the symbiosis described by the Argentine psychoanalyst Jose Bleger (1922–72), provoking an immobilization of this anxiety. We would thus oscillate between two sides of a splitting of the Ego, with, on the one hand, moments of awareness and, on the other hand, denial of our destructiveness and its infantile sources.

2   an "*environmental melancholy*" imposing itself in our relationship to this "hyperobject" that is the ecosystem, resulting in a hatred towards our fraternal and generational rivals: other species, animals and plants, future generations but also towards this "nourishing milk" which is the resources of the ecosystem that we squander. This destructive hatred could give rise to secondary guilt and a feeling of emptiness as an effect of our murderous activity.

(p. 201)

These two relevant hypotheses draw Bion's psychoanalytic concepts towards a new social theory based on post-Kleinian psychoanalysis; however, it seems to me that they do not question, or question very little, the limits of the psychoanalytic theories.

The purpose of this book is therefore to gather together some elements (some of them already developed in more detail in a recent book, Matot, 2019) to propose a conception of humanity that cannot be disconnected from its environment. This implies a distancing from a "naturalist" ontology (Descola, 2005) that is predominant in Western societies, based on the subject/object separation inherited from Enlightenment philosophy. Indeed, since this ontology tends, with the globalization of financial capitalism, to impose itself as a unique modality of the relationship between Man and his environment, it produces a vision of a totalitarian world that leads humankind to its loss.

It seems necessary to me to put the concept of a "natural" human envelope back into the core of our vision of Man; from this viewpoint, it is no longer possible to reduce environmental challenges to "relationships" between Man and his environment but to set this question in terms of the relationships between the various envelopes of human beings, whose consciousness is related to ontology and culture.

With such a change of epistemological markers, what role can psychoanalysis play in the emergence of a new human-environment ecosystemic paradigm? Psychoanalysis has developed fertile hypotheses and models that should allow it to make useful contributions to the understanding of what is at stake, for our humanity, in the understanding of the current ecosystem disaster. But, on the one hand, these hypothesis and models come from a time when this disaster was not yet thinkable, and, on the other hand, for more than half a century, a few voices – including that of the American psychoanalyst Harold Searles (1918–2015) – have risen to warn us of this occurrence, without any real interest from psychoanalytic circles.

Psychoanalysis grew within the Western vision of Man and world inherited from Enlightenment philosophy and founded, like the whole of European scientific thought, on a subject/object separation constitutive of what Descola, anthropologist, holder of the Chair of "Anthropology of Nature" at the College de France, designates "naturalist" ontology. As he points out in his book *Beyond Nature and Culture* (2005): "the modern West's way of representing nature is by no means widely shared. In many regions of the planet, humans and nonhumans are not conceived as developing in incommunicable worlds or according to quite separate principles" (p. 30). Descola distinguishes four major axes of anthropological construction of the being-man: animism, totemism, naturalism and analogism.

The "naturalist" anchoring of psychoanalysis constitutes today an important obstacle to understanding the apathy of our societies faced with the ecosystem disaster. The consumerist and managerial ideology of financial capitalism, whose "globalization" is responsible for this disaster, represents the extreme point of the naturalist ontology, where it becomes destructive of humanity.

In order to give itself the means to reflect on this essential problematic, psychoanalysis needs to reconsider the way it deals with this ontological separation between subject and object. This can be done starting from the issue inside/outside but requires reconsideration of how psychoanalytic theories build models of what we call "internal reality" on the basis of an unthought "external reality".

Failing such a problematization, I believe that psychoanalysts condemn themselves to missing the question of the Human–environment complex and, as Jacques Press (2019a) points out, to "export without distance theories resulting from their daily work into a field that is heterogeneous to theirs" and to "thus add confusion instead of producing creative thought" (p. 261). He notes in this respect the fundamental difference that must be taken into account between the early relationship of the baby to his objects of attachment, and the relationship of the human to his *Umwelt*, but indicates what for him connects them both: the effect on humans of the breakup of the stable and resistant framework on which his sense of being is built. The other point on which Press insists is the cut-off of the direct link between Man and his objects, in particular with those he produces or transforms through his economic activity. We are here at the heart of the problem highlighted by Descola's work.

Part I

An ecosystemic perspective

1 From the localization of the human psyche to the concepts of disseminated self and psychic envelopes

The four main lines of anthropological construction of the human being – animism, totemism, naturalism and analogism – differentiated by Descola allow us to better consider the "social" components of the identification processes of individuals, groups and cultures.

These four modes do not put the differences from which the world is structured in *Weltanschauungen* in the same places. They constitute

> schemas for integrating experience, which make it possible to structure, in a selective fashion, the flux of perceptions and relations. They do this by noting resemblances and differences between things on the basis of the same resources that every human carries within himself or herself: namely a body and intentionality.
>
> (Descola, 2005, pp. 232–3)

The many variants of these four identification modes, the mixing and the intermediaries they allow, foster the wealth of cultures:

> One or another of these modes of identification certainly becomes dominant in this or that historical situation and is consequently preferred and mobilized both in practical activities and in classificatory judgments, although this does not prevent the three other modes from sometimes infiltrating the formation of a representation, the organization of a course of action, or even the definition of a field of customs.
>
> (Descola, 2005, p. 233)

Descola's standpoint allows both relativizing the place of the "naturalist" mode, which organizes most Western societies, but also comprehending that at the most "meta" level of the identity constructs of mankind, the opposition of inside/outside on which they are based not only is not homogeneous but is also divided into several levels, structuring in various ways the domains of individual and collective spheres within different "environments" defined as such.

The importance of Descola's work lies in the fact that it highlights the consistent aspect and the internal coherence of other ways of apprehending the world than the one designed by "naturalist" ontology. He points out that while some of the responses of naturalism

> have a universal application – human rights and scientific procedures, for instance – but it is illusory to think that they can definitely resolve questions that are formulated in other places and in other contexts and that concern mysteries not even suspected.
>
> (Descola, 2005, p. 282)

This remark can, however, be complemented by the idea, found in Descola's work, that in every man, behind the predominant mode of comprehending the world to which he relates and the stalemates of collective organizations, other modes that reflect heterogeneous dimensions of individual psychism, collective phenomena and social functioning remain active and identifiable. How these alternative modes manifest and coexist in each individual and different societies is crucial in our individual and institutional relationships to ourselves and to the world.

If, as I believe, with Descola, "the naturalist schema can no longer be taken for granted . . . and a phase of ontological recomposition may be beginning" (2005, p. 198), the ways of thinking of the human in the different fields of knowledge, in particular in that of psychoanalysis, will have to open up to new paradigms to avoid the risk of obsolescence.

> Anthropology is thus faced with a daunting challenge: either to disappear as an exhausted form of humanism, or else to transform itself by rethinking its domain and its tools in such a way as to include in its object far more than the Anthropos: that is to say, the entire collective of beings that is linked to him but that is at present relegated to the position of a merely peripheral role.
>
> (Descola, 2005, p. XX)

Descola writes in the preface of his book. Probably the same is true for psychoanalysis.

Sigmund Freud thought, not without ambivalence, that the future of psychoanalysis would lie in the advances of science. However, the idea that the human psyche resides in the brain and, by extension, in the body that allows it to function, is now being re-evaluated even in the field of academic medicine. In his book *La sculpture du vivant* (1999, re-edition 2003), Jean-Claude Ameisen, a French immunologist, ethicist and outstanding popularizer of advances in biology but also a critical and creative thinker of the issues raised by the progress of biomedical sciences, invites us to rethink the concepts of body and body envelope.

Studying the "functions" of living organisms, Ameisen points out, using the example of the development of the immune system, that

> the nature of the consequences of the presence of an organ, a structure, a shape, a protein . . . depends entirely on the interior and exterior environment of this body. The idea of function is inseparable from the notion of context. What we usually call a function is, among the countless possible modalities of living self-organization, one of the observable consequences of a random and singular crystallization of which the stability and durability have been favoured at some point by external constraints which constantly put pressure on the community of cells, proteins and genes that make up the individuals of a species. Should the context change, the "function" will change.
>
> (2003, p. 251)

So, bodily functions express a particular state of the potential of the relationship between an organism and its environment. It seems to me that it is only in a very reductive fashion that we can describe them as "properties" of this organism: they are just as much the "properties" of the surroundings of this organism.

In another chapter of his book, Ameisen starts from the study of a unicellular eukaryotic organism, *Trypanosoma cruzi*, a permanent parasite of two categories of hosts, insects and mammals, which takes, depending on the host and its location, three different forms: epimastigote in insects, amastigote in humans, both of which can either split locally or give birth to a trypomastigote, which does not split but travels from one host to another. These transformations take place by cellular differentiation. To take these different forms, *T. cruzi* only activates part of its genetic heritage.

The epimastigotes, growing in the upper part of the digestive tract of the insect, form a compact colony; when they pass through the lower part of the digestive tract, they self-destruct when they find themselves at some distance from one another: they need signals from their peers to develop. The only alternative to self-destruction lies in the transformation, for some of them, into trypomastigotes. Thus, *Trypanosoma cruzi* constitutes, in its three forms of existence, separated by apoptosis "phases", "a complex society relocated in time and space" (Ameisen, 2003, p. 260):

> The cycle of metamorphoses of *T. cruzi* . . . does not create an embryo as we normally understand it. But it has its essential characteristics: cell differentiation, cell migration, geographic and temporal distribution of

offspring, and cell suicide as an alternative to differentiation and migration. It is a peculiar form of "embryonic development", which spawns gives birth to a peculiar form of body. . . . Epimastigotes in insects and amastigotes in humans are very similar to the somatic cells that build and compose our bodies and will disappear with us. Trypomastigotes are like germinal cells . . . that build new cell societies.

(Ameisen, 2003, p. 261)

Ameisen provides an even more disturbing example, the case of another unicellular, *Dictyostelium discoidum*, a mould that forms by duplication a colony that extends over the surface of the ground. When the surroundings become unfavourable, some single-cell organisms begin to send out chemical signals that attract their fellow creatures in concentric waves, first by spirals in a single file, then, when their density increases, by attaching themselves to each other, gradually constituting a compact body of several hundred thousand microorganisms moving like a slug which, after 24 hours, rises vertically from the ground, like a tiny flower measuring only a few millimetres. The signals that initiated this mass grouping behaviour cause two types of cellular transformations: a part of the cells die to form the rigid stem of the body, and another part turns into resistant spores, clustered into a spheric shape at the top of the stem. When the environment becomes favourable again, the spores turn into active cells that will split to reform a colony of unicellular microorganisms.

Thus, Ameisen's thoughts lead him to the idea that a function corresponds to a system of interactions between a set of potentials of an organ (or a structure) and a set of features of this organ's (or structure's) environment. A function is what links the features of an organism to those of its environment to produce specific effects necessary to its survival, its development and its reproduction.

What in psychoanalysis we refer to as "Ego functions", in other words, the combination of all the skills acquired within this fictitious entity that, since Freud, we call the "Ego", can also be considered functions of a "Ego-environment" system. We can assume that the development of the object of psychoanalysis led to reducing to only one of the two terms, consistent with the illusion of an autonomous human "body" as a result of a set of "functions" developed within it.

In the same way, the concept of "body" revisited by Ameisen allows us to go beyond the conception of an Ego related to an inside-outside separation, corresponding to the bodily envelope. Observing the existence of apoptosis in several microorganisms such as *T. cruzi* led him to conceive that a "body", defined as an interdependent functional set of cells with minimal differentiation and specialization between them, contributing to the survival of the species and its reproduction, can be located in different spaces and times.

The specialization of cells, as we know, is closely linked to their environment. The life cycle of the cells and of the "body" they form also varies according to changes in the environment on two levels: on the one hand, the environment constituted by the other cells of the "body", which communicate with each other by means of chemical (and then also electrical) signals and, on the other hand, in close interaction with this level, let's say "groupal", the "non-cellular" environment, temperatures, availability of water and oxygen, of nutrients. . . . By analogy, we have to conceive of the Human "environment" embracing, on the one hand, relationships within human groups and, on the other hand, institutions, cultures and their ecosystems.

The set of functions that regulates human life can thus be seen as unfolding in and out of our bodily envelope; some functions are purely "internal", others are purely "external" and a whole series of others are both "internal" and "external". Among these, some are supported by the differentiation inside/outside; others are more or less unaware of it (we could call them "transitional" or intermediate). Very fast technological developments considerably increase the variety, power and diffusion of these intermediate functions.

The functions involving the differentiation of inside/outside supported by the bodily envelope correspond roughly to those of the Freudian Ego. Didier Houzel (1987), a French psychoanalyst influenced by post-Kleinian psychoanalysis currents, points out that, in Freud's works, "the issue of a structure containing and limiting the psyche . . . takes the form of the concept of 'Ego'" (p. 25). However, the focus of psychoanalysis on the intra-psychic topic has reinforced the illusion of an autonomous "existence" of this Ego, which for Freud is based from the outset on taking for granted the presence of a "caring environment", meaning not only the "primary maternal concern" and the "good enough" mother, upon which Winnicott insisted later, but also a "non-human" caring environment.

It therefore seems necessary to me that psychoanalysis thinks of another instance, broader than the Freudian Ego, which it would encompass as one of its functional units, taking into account the spread-out space, not limited by the bodily envelope, within which different types of human functions are displayed. This perspective brings back to the forefront the concept of plurality of psychic envelopes that was particularly developed by French psychoanalysts, especially Didier Houzel, already quoted, but also René Kaës, whose works on the groupal envelope (1976) and unconscious alliances (2010) have opened up new theoretical and clinical spaces for psychoanalysis.

The concept of "Self" – associated with the term "disseminated" – seems to me appropriate to express the idea that the limits of Human are merged with what everyone sees as "external reality" and thereby radically differentiate this concept of Self from other meanings in which it has been previously used. As a "container" of the plurality of human psychic envelopes, the Disseminated Self also reflects the need, in order to correctly apprehend the human phenomenon, its avatars and in particular the destruction of our ecosystem, to conceptualize a "body-environment" system in which these two terms are inseparable. Such a notion sheds new light on Winnicott's assertion that the subjective experience of the baby initially includes "two" mothers: the mother who is the object of the drive and the "mother-environment". The "mother-environment" is the primitive unit from which the instinctive experiences of the baby with the "mother-object of the drive" gradually allow the differentiation between inside/outside and the constitution of the Ego. According to Winnicott, these "two" mothers are part of the baby's subjective experience when coming into the "depressive position" thought through by the Austrian-born British psychoanalyst Melanie Klein (1882–1960). But this integration does not, in my opinion, make the "mother-environment" level of experience disappear; on the contrary, it becomes the background supporting the instinctual life and the container for the PS/D oscillation described by Bion (1962).

Given the "Disseminated Self" as a "container", I would like to point out that the concept of psychic envelope, even if it has the advantage of offering an intermediate representation of the disseminated nature of our psychism, still has a misleading spatial – and even visual – connotation that we will have to go beyond to better understand the nature of human functioning.

In his article *"Le concept d'enveloppe psychique"* (1987), Didier Houzel insists on its metaphorical meaning. He defines the psychic envelope as "the boundary between inner and outer world, between the inner psychic world of the psychic world of others" (p. 24). He broadens the perspective by emphasizing that the term "envelope" – especially when an analogy with the skin is made – can induce a simplistic, anatomical view of the concept. "The psychic envelope must not be conceived in a static way, but rather as a dynamic system . . . [it] could be compared to a force field". Houzel (2010) further discusses the issue of psychic envelopes in an original and fruitful way, focusing his approach on their key function, that is, to stabilize psychic functioning. He finds the origins of this perspective in Freud's early work *Project for a Scientific Psychology* (1895), in which Freud "defines the Ego as the part of the psychic apparatus that has acquired a stable level of energy and tends to return to that level when it is energized" (Houzel, 2010, p. 13). Referring to the mathematician René Thom's work, Houzel considers the structural stability in a dynamic system, here the "stabilization of drive

motions and emotional turbulences". Struggle against overflowing and dis-
organization is a never-ending task for the psyche. At the beginning of life,
"the caring environment" takes on this task "to calm the turbulences and
stabilize the system it constitutes with the starving baby". Houzel leads us
to the idea that, without sufficient structural stability, the psyche withdraws
to a simple, nondynamic stability, based on the maintenance of the identical: "The lowest level of stability is the complete absence of movement, the
suppression of any change, of any evolution. . . . This is the level of stability
to which Freud refers to define the death instinct" (Houzel, 2010, p. 17).
The child's game, such as the compulsion to repeat – which also includes the
pleasure principle – must be considered from this perspective. During the
early months, it is not the action "on" the baby that Houzel points out but
the action within the baby–environment system. The role of the mother, or
of the person who provides mothering care, is of course essential and has
rightly been the object of theoretical works by Anglo-Saxon psychoanalysts, from Klein to Winnicott and Bion. However, we must broaden our
approach to all the components of the baby's environment, animate and
inanimate, even if the quality of the primary maternal concern (Winnicott)
or the mother's capacity for reverie (Bion) occupy a central and organizational place in – and of – this complex. Houzel emphasizes that birth, in
other words, the end of intrauterine life, introduces a discontinuity between
the experience of need and that of its satisfaction: "from that moment on, a
gradient is created between the nascent infant's Self and its libidinal object"
(2010, p. 19). This gradient creates a dynamic gap, "a field of attraction that
draws the Self to the object with irrepressible strength. The violence of this
attraction is a source of turbulence and threatens the Self with loss of coherence and destruction".

Unlike Houzel, the model I propose considers a range of psychic envelopes (and not just a single one, made up of several sheets, as he proposes
in his work on autism). According to this model, the human psyche could
be conceived as a set of operations-organizations, which I call "configurations", each generating a specific psychic envelope. These "configurations-
envelopes" would be invested-activated-disinvested-deactivated at different
times to meet the needs of the "Disseminated Self". With this concept, I am
referring to the systemic corpus specific to each "human entity", constituted
by these "envelopes" – or, in the model I propose, "psychic configurations" –
and the transitions from one to another.

This idea of a variety of envelopes/configurations corresponding to different levels of organization of the psyche seems to me already present in
the description that Didier Anzieu (1985) gives of a more archaic topic,
perhaps primal, pre-existent to the Self: the sense of being of the Self. For
him, this Self corresponds to the sound and olfactory envelope, outside

of which both endogenous and exogenous stimuli are projected. The Self grows by introjection of the infants' surroundings, first sounds (but also flavours and odours), as a pre-individual psychic container endowed with an outline of unity and identity (Anzieu, 1985, p. 159). The Self proposed by Anzieu develops like a sound envelope by experiencing ambient sounds during breastfeeding. This sound environment previews the Ego-Skin and its double face turned inward and outward. . . . This combination of sounds produces: a) a common space-volume allowing bilateral exchange, b) a first image (spatio-auditory) of the infant body and c) a close realization bond with the mother (Anzieu, 1985, pp. 168–9).

Anzieu sees sound space as the first psychic space . . . it is a sheltered space but not tightly sealed. It is followed by the visual space, the visual-tactile space, the locomotor space and finally by the graphic space. Anzieu hypothesizes that the Ego differentiates itself by encompassing this original Self, starting with the tactile experience, which allows the establishment of limits and boundaries of the Ego as a two-dimensional interface. Anzieu completes his hypothesis by stating that the secondary topic (Id, Ego, Superego) is organized when the visual envelope – especially under the effect of the primary prohibition of touch – replaces the tactile envelope. According to him, this corresponds to the development of the Preconscious, when the representations of things (mainly visual) are associated with representations of words (provided by the acquisition of speech). Anzieu points out that in this model, there is a sound mirror that predates the visual mirror, which means that the reflexive function could be present very early, before language acquisition.

The dynamic perspective of psychic envelopes (which for me are a metaphoric way of approaching the complex nature of the idea of "psychic configurations") makes it possible to conceive a variety of human envelopes, group envelopes (Anzieu, 1984; Kaës, 1976), technological envelopes (Leroi-Gourhan, 1943, 1945; Stiegler, 1994), institutional and social envelopes (Bleger, 1967). But we must go further in our questioning in order to clarify the nature of the relationship between the Disseminated Self and the environment.

2 About the transformational potential of non-differentiation

The challenge is therefore to reexamine the psychoanalytic models based on the oppositions: subject/object, Ego/Non Ego, inside/outside, internal reality/external reality. In order to do this, I think it is interesting to start with the Kantian concept of the unknowable nature "the thing in itself", Lacan's "Real", Winnicott's "unformed", Bleger's "ambiguity", Bion's "O" and, more broadly, with anything that attempts to account for non-differentiation (which, with Winnicott, it is necessary to distinguish from loss of differentiation that occurs as a defence against differentiations threatening the sense of identity).

Freud, while endorsing the Kantian proposal of an unknowable real, nevertheless circumscribed the field of psychoanalysis to the study of an "internal reality", psychic, confronted with an "external reality", hence reified.

When he rejects the idea of a psychoanalytical *Weltanschauung*, to inscribe psychoanalysis in the field of scientific thinking, Freud (1933) explains that "our best hope for the future is that intellect – the scientific spirit, reason – may in process of time establish a dictatorship in the mental life of man" (S.E., 22, p. 170). Indeed, he writes,"its endeavor is to arrive at correspondence with reality, that is to say, with what exists outside of us, independently of us. . . . This correspondence with the real external world, we call 'truth'" (22, p. 169). However, this formulation assumes that reality is always a psychic construct and that this concordance with the "real" can only be approached without ever being reached. However, Freud does not consider the issue of the intractable gap between aspiration for an "equivalence with the real external world" and the impossibility of establishing it; he "forgets" it and acts as if "external" reality could be considered an invariant of experience.

While Freud admits that totemism and animism (which he curiously equates to "a time without religion", p. 163) have not disappeared, he sees them only as superstitions. So, it seems that the construction of psychoanalysis found itself trapped, because of Freud's personal positions – of course partly related to his time – between an objectifying scientistic vision of material reality and a psychologizing theory of social functioning based on his "oedipal" psychoanalytic hypotheses. By reducing religions, remnants "of ignorant times during the dawn of humankind", to "a counterpart of the neurosis through which the civilized individual must pass on his journey from childhood to maturity" (p. 167), by rebelling against "this obscure Hegelian philosophy, school through which Marx also passed" (p. 176) and by clinging to a "colonial" view of the dominating economic and political relationships ("social distinctions, so I thought, were originally distinctions between clans or races", p. 176), Freud has built a psychoanalysis with a line of vision from which a large area of the psychism was amputated, that is, that which is intimately entangled with "external reality" that he himself stated as invariant.

Freud's position is understandable and was probably necessary for the invention of psychoanalysis: in order to carry out an epistemological revolution, one needs to find a fixed point to anchor it: it was "external reality". But, as Delaunoy (1989) points out, this position is unsustainable, and it is very surprising that, since Freud, most psychoanalysts continue to act as if the notion of external reality was not a problem.

The time has come for psychoanalysis to confront this paradox: on the one hand, mankind needs to think an "outside" in order to allow identifying himself with an "inside". The concepts of "reality" and "environment" fulfil this function. But, on the other hand, the evolutions of societies, under the partly combined effects of ultraliberal ideologies and technological advances, have highlighted what previously remained barely mentioned and could be neglected: Human's psyche is by nature intimately intricated with what Searles (1960) called the "non-human", and this intricacy is both conscious and unconscious. Today, the development of digital identities and existences, the complexification of man/woman differentiations, perhaps even parent/child, tomorrow, relations that Man will have with "intelligent" machines that are getting closer and closer but also the developments in genomics and non-sexual reproduction of humans compel us and will compel us more and more to make room in our conceptions and theories of the Human to this "external" reality that must be fully recognized as psychic in order to be subjectively appropriated by human beings.

The Disseminated Self and the psychic configurations, viewed as a set of differentiations inside/outside, is worth exploring to resolve this paradox. But these differentiations, on which individuals and societies build their identities, can only be formed from a raw material of non-differentiation. In order for anything to take shape, it still needs a gross material that can be transformed.

Winnicott is probably the psychoanalyst who acknowledged the most the prerequisite necessity of the unformed, without which no form can occur. Maybe one should point out that which is only implicit in his articles: the unformed is continually renewed in our psyche, as an indispensable source of our vitality and creativity and of the effectiveness of our symbolization processes.

Apart from psychoanalysis and artistic creation, this question, as well as the one about our relationship to technical objects, was covered in a fruitful and original way by the French philosopher and psychologist Gilbert Simondon (1924–89). His work on individuation processes (1958, 2005), inspired by thermodynamics of states far from equilibrium, quantum physics and cybernetics, puts the "pre-individual" potential at the core of individuation. Moreover, he extends these processes from human to technical individuals, each one of them inscribed, as André Leroi-Gourhan (1943, 1945) had already shown, in evolutionary lineages.

For Simondon, individuation occurs because of the saturation that takes place in a system that he describes as pre-individual – which I assimilate with the concepts of non-differentiation and unformed – leading to the emergence, in the same movement, of an individual and his environment. The obvious central point of this theory is that the individual does not "arrive" into a given environment but is "produced" by a differentiation process that constitutes at the same time what appears as an environment. This idea is also pivotal in Winnicott's thinking:

> I would say that before object relationships the state of affairs is this: that the unit is not the individual, the unit is an environment-individual set-up. The centre of gravity of the being does not start off in the individual. It is in the total set-up.
>
> (1952, p. 98)

For Simondon, groupal and collective identities emerge through the regression of individuals towards their pre-individual potential, which allows access to what he calls a "trans-individual" level and to its specific environment.

Using this model, I propose the concept of a "Self-environment" to account for both the persistence in each individual of a "pre-individual" matrix and the impossibility of considering human envelopes independently from the environment that appears as such due to each differentiation process.

This "pre-individual" that Simondon places at the origin of the processes of differentiation and individuation can be put in perspective, in the field of psychoanalytic theories, with the concepts of "unformed" and "non-differentiation" used by Winnicott but also with the concept of "ambiguity" used by the Argentine psychoanalyst José Bleger (1922–72). The latter's developments on the syncretic parts of the psyche immobilized in and by the inanimate setting (1967) allow us to address the catastrophic anxieties mobilized by fractures of our life "frames" – including the anxiety of loss of container caused by migratory phenomena (De Micco, 2019) or the impact on our lifestyles of the fight against actual viral pandemics. However, Bleger does not distinguish between loss of differentiation and non-differentiation. It seems to me that the perspective he opens offers more opportunities – and is more optimistic – by assuming that the inanimate setting also "contains", alongside "de-differentiated" parts (which he identifies as "psychotic") that are potential sources of catastrophic anxiety, a whole potential of non-differentiation which may contribute to new processes of differentiation and symbolization. We will come back to this later.

Beforehand, to complete the heuristic value of Simondon's work towards a theory of "the outside", I would like to emphasize the importance he attaches to the evolution of technical individuals – and to their constitution as technological collectives – in their relation to the evolution of human societies. It is not necessary to demonstrate the major impact of the developments of information technology and digital tools on our connected lives, but it is important that psychoanalytic theories of symbolization take this into account. My proposition is to consider, alongside the primary and secondary forms of symbolization that have been identified and worked on, a tertiary symbolization, which involves not only the use of technical objects but the intricacy of our existence with that of these objects. Our digital "existences" and "traces" are a prevailing first manifestation of this, but it is quite obvious that this movement will grow and gain increasingly wide territories of our psyches.

3 Destructiveness, omnipotence, rest . . .

The importance that should therefore be given to non-differentiation and the unformed, extending Winnicott's pioneering work, sheds light on the individual but above all collective and cultural defensive systems which prevent Human from perceiving the vital continuity which unites him to his environment and from feeling as his own the deep wounds that he inflicts upon it, that he lets be perpetrated and that he ultimately inflicts to himself.

The problem lies in the conception of the core of what we call "environment". Is it an outside, with which we maintain projective relations, an "other" object, in a way of thinking based on the distinction between subject and object? Or is it, again and again, necessarily, a part of our psyche? This seems to me to be a major issue. It echoes Winnicott's 1963 criticism of Harold Searles' early book, *The Non-Human Environment* (1960):

> It seems that his term is not good enough. . . . I think Searles is referring to the non-projective environment, or all those aspects of the individual's environment that in fact take effect or impinge before the individual baby is ready to gain control of external reality by the mechanisms of projection and introjection. . . . The early oneness of the stage before the baby separates off the mother from the self, that which appears in psychotic illness as a merging, is a oneness not with a person, nor with an object; it is a oneness with the non-human environment, or, as I would like to call it, a non-projective environment.
>
> (Winnicott, 1989, p. 480)

It is indeed decisive, in order to reflect on the destruction of our ecosystem and the means to transform our relationship to this "environment" constitutive of our humanity, to consider the double polarity of the conception that Human has of his environment: on the one hand, an "external world" object of projections; on the other hand, intrinsic unity to his very nature.

In the field of psychoanalysis, Winnicott was the first to outline a middle path that strongly linked differentiation processes to retaining an intermediate space of non-differentiation, which he called "transitional". I support the need to extend this heuristic hypothesis, which makes it possible to avoid the reification of a true/false, inside/outside logic by viewing psychic functioning as unfolding and investing a number of levels of organization corresponding to heterogeneous psychic spaces and plural modalities of relationship between the individual and his worlds.

Such a hypothesis seems to me to agree with Descola's (2005) anthropological perspective mentioned at the beginning of the present book, underpinning a vision of humans inseparable from the ontological axes (naturalist, animist, totemic and analogical) he proposes to approach the great diversity of cultures, ways of living and of being.

The "globalization" induced by the worldwide hegemony of the ideology of financial capitalism tends to make this plurality disappear, relegated to a status of exotic curiosity by the imperialism of its values and the omnipresence of its norms: absolute primacy of capital gains over ecosystem stability, monopolistic appropriation of techniques that accelerate the reduction of human beings to their market value by the double effect of the consumerist "ideal" and managerial violence.

Destruction of human beings with their environment by the pervasiveness of hyper-capitalist culture so appears as what it is: a "soft genocide", beside the human genocides and the exclusion of a majority of mankind from social welfare, health and techniques. This clearly shows that "culture" cannot merely be seen in terms of a "legacy" of childhood transitional phenomena, as Winnicott suggested, but must also be considered in terms of the social destructiveness that it generates, as emphasized by Freud (1930) in *Civilization and Its Discontents*. In this respect, I am struck by the number of books that nowadays deal with the mechanisms of social destruction of the Nazi system: *Berlin Noir* (Kerr P., 1994), followed by Philip Kerr's latest novel, *Prussian Blue* (2017); *L'ordre du jour* by Eric Vuillard (2017); *Les amnésiques* by Géraldine Schwartz (2019); and Edith Sheffer's *Asperger's Children* (2018), to name but a few, and, in the field of psychoanalysis, essays by Kostas Nassikas ("*Exils de langue*" 2011) and by Laurence Kahn ("*Ce que le nazisme a fait à la psychanalyse*" 2018). They all tell us about the relevance of the destructiveness of ideologies and human organizations for mankind in these times of ecosystem genocide.

Freud, however, started thinking along a path – followed after him by many psychoanalysts who tried to theorize "the problem of evil" – of a dialectic between "life instincts" and "death instincts" and within the framework of a monolithic psychic topic, Id/Superego/Ego, based on a somewhat static conception of the relationship between "internal reality" and "external reality".

In this respect, the opposition retained by Bleger, but also theorized by Bion, between psychotic and non-psychotic parts of the personality, certainly seems to offer a heuristic model to conceive, for the former, the risks due to the breaking up of our social, institutional and individual frameworks and, for the latter, thought disorders. However, this dual approach appears to me today an obstacle to further theorization of the transitional potential of the psyche. Indeed, speaking of psychotic parts tends to give legitimacy to the idea – even if it does not necessarily correspond to Bion's ideas, for example – of areas of the psyche referred to as psychotic, of which the contribution to personal and collective creativity would be reduced or nil. This opposition, which again appears as a legacy of "naturalist" ontology, tends to freeze perspectives that do not take into consideration that the potential for creativity and/or destructiveness of mental functioning depends on the psychic states in which they occur. This insight seems obvious for the dream; it is even at the root of the Freudian theory:

> We are not in the habit of devoting much thought to the fact that every night human beings lay aside the wrappings in which they have enveloped their skin. . . . We may add that when they go to sleep they carry out an entirely analogous undressing of their minds and lay aside most of their psychical acquisitions.
>
> (Freud, 1915)

This insight, however, is not so easily accepted for the whole variety of psychic states we go through in our daily life, in line with the issues and the "tasks" that occupy us. It is, however, obvious for artists, painters, musicians, writers. Winnicott made it central to his conception of the mother's primary bond with her baby, the "primary maternal preoccupation", which he says would be considered "psychotic" if it did not occur in this very particular phase of motherhood.

From this viewpoint, the recent analysis that the Swiss psychoanalyst Luc Magnenat (2019) proposes of the destructiveness underlying the apathy about the ecosystem disaster, confronting psychotic and non-psychotic parts of the personality linked to transformational or obstructive modalities of the primary ties to parents (pp. 180–2), should be broadened. In addition to removing the potential for indeterminacy that, I think, remains throughout life in connection with the zones of non-differentiation that remain potentially active, such a dual dialectic does not take sufficient account of the levels of differentiation inside/outside and of the plurality of *vertexes* where the various expressions of destructiveness manifest.

I think of a patient who tells me that she dreamt that her husband was flirting with a very pretty woman in their living room, while she herself was sleeping in their bedroom. In her dream, she is overcome by frenzied rage and murderous desires. When she wakes up, she sees her husband sleeping next to her. Her rage does not subside; she is under extreme tension and ends up waking him up to accuse him of wanting to sleep with another woman in their house in her presence, which triggers a violent row. The violence of affects in the dream space is not transformed by the awakening; the topical differentiations are superimposed in both spaces, on a hallucinatory continuum, making an intermediate transitional functioning and the passage from one level of reality to another temporarily inaccessible. What I describe as a passage from one psychic configuration to another is impeded, which maintains an untransformed violent expression that the patient experiences as "insane".

Transposed to an awareness of the urgency of collective action to address the climate crisis, this example illustrates that the concept of splitting is inadequate and misleading to understand what is at stake. It is necessary to consider the levels of reality within which the experience is felt and transformed.

Destructiveness is not of the same nature, does not involve the same issues and does not require the same remedies, depending on whether it operates in non-differentiated or in differentiated and de-differentiated zones.

From the standpoint of the destructiveness that is experienced within the zones of non-differentiation, handed down from the primary unit baby-environment, it belongs to what Winnicott called "cruel primary love". The remedy he prescribed is the capacity of the environment to survive (Winnicott, 1971) this cruelty and to transform it within a relationship that, through a double movement of giving limits (recognition of the pain caused by cruelty and limits to the expression of this cruelty) and of offering an alternative outcome to the vitality that is expressed as cruelty and enables us to develop creativity, that is, the ability to broaden, through our experiences, the space in which we live and in which our abilities to act unfold.

From the standpoint of projective destructiveness (which I would qualify as "secondary" because it operates in the field of inside/outside differentiations), linked to the projection of the "bad" outside and to the omnipotent control that we try to maintain over what is expelled from our "inside", it is still – according to Winnicott – the issue of reparation that remains central. Projective destructiveness can only be transformed when the depressive position (conceptualized by Melanie Klein) – or capacity for concern (Winnicott) – has been reached, opening the way to awareness of guilt, concern for others and an authentic capacity for repair.

Here is where the interplay between the two "remedies" appears: indeed, access to the depressive position is conditioned by sufficient transformation of the cruelty of primary love.

Thus, personalities that are built on a lack of transformation of primary cruelty are characterized by an indifference to the damage caused to an environment which is defensively experienced as infinitely indestructible. Indeed, this indifference appears as a radical protection against an intolerable threat of annihilation of the primary unit.

In personalities where guilt and the capacity for repair have been better integrated into the personality, it is possible to rely on these attainments to counteract and contain projective destructiveness.

In the first instance, anything that tends to rationally demonstrate the destructive impact of the human way of life is inaudible and intolerable and can therefore only be subject to radical rejection and denial. It is not a coincidence that this type of negationism brings together in the same hatred the advocates of climate change scepticism and xenophobic stigmatization of foreigners and migrants. The only way to calm down and socially contain this destructive rage is both to set a firm but non-excluding limit to individuals and groups who are prisoners of these behaviours (and especially avoid electing them for public responsibilities) and to invent adequate and gratifying forms of socializing their rage: it should be possible, with a little imagination and tolerance, to invent something other than the Foreign Legion . . . or Daesh. . . .

In the second instance, the repair capacity is more accessible. Many individuals and groups are already moving in this direction, and most fields of knowledge are contributing to it through new research.

One important point when dealing with destructiveness at a societal level is to take into account the daily violence, related to social pressure, people experience in their lives.

> An airport, summer departure day. A journalist interviews some holidaymakers about the importance of environmental concerns in choosing to travel by air. A passenger begins by defensively arguing that a plane does not pollute more than lines of cars stuck in endless traffic jams; then she gets upset: "I work hard all year round and I'm exhausted, I need these holidays to chill out, to clear my head, it's perfectly normal, isn't it?"

The issue of the radical transformations of Western lifestyles that would be required to significantly reduce ecosystem destruction and depletion of natural resources is crucial in assessing the apathy about the environment. This passenger's answer is very meaningful in this respect: it underlines the strong link between the deleterious effects that the exploitation of human life and work has on the sense of well-being and health and the consumerist "reward" that is supposed to compensate for the psychological and physical cost of this existential alienation.

This link questions the future and avatars of our omnipotence. Until recently, Man has considered his "natural environment" as globally as unalterable as it is eternal. Of course, he had to take into account the "whims" of nature, sometimes with devastating consequences for him, but it only reinforced the idea of an indestructible and permanent environment, set against his own vulnerability and ephemeral condition.

Winnicott described the way in which the mother, at the birth of her baby, is in a state that he qualified as "primary maternal concern": the maternal psyche includes the newborn in a baby-environment unit that adjusts as closely as possible to the infant's needs because of a psychic permeability to the baby's internal states. This "winnicottian" baby then experiences a form of primary omnipotence, which goes hand in hand with his ignorance of the absolute dependence that makes it possible. Winnicott sees in this omnipotence the deep roots of creativity, a concept that for him does not refer to something exceptional, such as artistic creation, but rather to an ability to simply live one's life creatively. Then, very quickly, in line with the rapid development of the baby's skills, the mother gradually moves away from this "primary concern" to become the "good enough" mother that Winnicott talks about, a mother who gradually reinvests the "outside" of this baby-environment unit. She allows her child to progressively move out of this primary omnipotence, becoming capable of more and more subtle discriminations, developing his ability to anticipate and integrate temporality, delay, small frustrations. The processes of symbolization, fed by the "infantile sexuality", namely the pleasure taken in the intertwining of body functions, the attention of parents and others and emotional exchanges, deepen the associative, play and representational capacities and constitute the driving force behind the transformation of omnipotence. But this is only possible insofar as there is vitality. Rest manifests as an awakened state of relaxation, of floating, of evanescence as spaces of omnipotence are also retained: such as space for play, space for daydreams, but also spaces for the formless, for "the nothing", which Winnicott refers to as the "rest" necessary to maintain thoughts . . . a pleasure that it is important to distinguish from the one related to the domain of Freudian sexuality, governing the differentiated zones of the psyche.

The other basic condition for the transformation of omnipotence is the possibility of feeling like an actor of one's own life, of appropriating it and living it in a way that can be felt as personal. Passivation, that is, the feeling of passively enduring an existence determined essentially by external constraints, leaves, as the only way out of omnipotence, the masochism of depression, rooted in melancholy nuclei, or the paranoid violence of narcissistic perversions.

These two basic conditions, availability to psychic states of rest and subjective appropriation, are precisely what the social organization established by the "hyper-capitalist culture" tends to eliminate. What remains, then, is the infinite quest for consumerist substitutes that close the loop and maintain what Rosa (2010), in his reflection on acceleration-related alienation, called the "hamster wheel". Or even what could be called psychosomatic exhaustion, nowadays readily categorized as "burn out", "fibromyalgia", "chronic fatigue syndrome" . . . medically socialized expressions of the symptomatic manifestations of our apathy.

Part II
Metapsychology

4   Psychic spaces and the topic of the Disseminated Self

Winnicott developed a notion of "three psychoanalyses" (Matot, 2014), a concept that is relatively understated in comparison to other parts of his work. This perspective gives legitimacy to the idea that therapeutic work with a given patient would tend to focus on a predominant modality of his relationship to himself and to the world at a vertex particularly related to the core of his pathology or suffering. This model was already apparent in 1945 in the article "Primary Emotional Development", but he explained it more thoroughly in 1954 in the article "The Metapsychological and Clinical Aspects of Regression within the Analytical Situation" (before taking it up again in "Human Nature", written in 1954, revised in 1967 and published after his death). To sum up, Winnicott distinguishes between so-called neurotic patients, who do not have very pronounced splitting mechanisms, for whom the classical Freudian technique would be appropriate; patients whose "Kleinian" issues involve the integration of love and hate and the awareness of dependence, for whom the elaboration of the depressive position is at the core of the therapeutic work, with, from the point of view of the psychoanalytic technique, the importance of the analyst's "survival"; and, finally, patients for whom the question of regression to dependence is at the core of the analytical work, in which the flaws of symbolization imply that acting out constitutes a mode of expression of the traumatic zones, soliciting action from the analyst to contain it and transform it by adapting the setting. About this last technical category, Winnicott reports a typical three-step sequence in his 1954 article: the analyst begins by tolerating the acting out; then, he tries to formulate what the patient sought to obtain from the analyst in this way, which brings to light the dynamics of deficiency situations in the primary environment; finally, either he resorts to "management", that is, to the adaptation of the analyst's behaviour, including aspects of the setting, in order not to reproduce a situation of intolerable deficiency, or he just tries to "survive" by bearing the patient's anger when he or she is confronted with the interpretation of repetition in the analysis of a situation of primary deficiency, highlighted by the acting out. Winnicott hypothesizes that

> the analyst may now have to take part by being used in respect of his failures rather than of his successes. This is disconcerting unless it is understood. The progress has been made through the analyst's very careful attempt at adaptation, and yet it is the failure that at this moment is singled out as important on account of its being a reproduction of the original failure or trauma.
>
> (1954, p. 288)

The aim is to manage to find the subtle proportion for an adaptation that is "good enough": too insufficient, and it repeats the traumatic intrusion without the possibility of transforming it; excessive, and the adaptation prevents the patient from coming into contact with his traumatic zones; almost sufficient, but not quite, allows the patient to rely on what is offered to him to experience what is lacking, to recognize it and to symbolize it.

The model that emerges over time in my practice relativizes such a proposition without excluding it: in standard cures, in particular, as a result of the frequency of sessions and the duration of the treatment, long periods are dominated by an elaboration that unfolds most of the time in a given psychic configuration. The technical guidelines provided by Winnicott, among others, are then very useful. However, the most obvious moments of transformation occur precisely when a configuration until then not constituted as such appears. In many psychoanalytical treatments that are practiced face to face or through other means like psychodrama, with a much reduced frequency and duration, the work on transitions from one psychological configuration to another can take up more space if, however, the analyst pays attention to them and has a theory that allows him or her to be receptive to them and to work with them.

The hypothesis on which I am working is therefore based on the idea that every human person functions in and between several psychic "spaces", more or less made one's own and subjectivated, which together form what I call the Disseminated Self.

These psychic "spaces" of the Disseminated Self belong to a set of "self-environment" configurations coming from the different differentiations – always partial and incomplete – of the primitive "baby-environment" unit posited in particular by Winnicott (1952). These "psychic configurations" are constituted by a set of psychosomatic functions playing the role of "attractors" agreeing with various perceptual-motor levels, phantasmatic organization and topical differentiation, beyond the limits of the body. In the theorization proposed by Houzel (1987), the "attractors" organize psychic areas, but the author emphasizes that the envelopes are not organized according to the temporo-spatial markers of the Euclidean space; in this, he agrees with Bion (1965) that the field of psychoanalytical objects cannot be limited to the model of the Euclidean space but must be conceived in the scope of multidimensionality.

Such a perspective postulates the existence, in the same individual, of a plurality of levels of differentiation inside/outside. It leads us to consider the in-depth study of the various dimensions of the psychic envelopes, which correspond to what the French philosopher Merleau-Ponty referred to as "the background unknown to me":

> "The spontaneous acts by which Man has shaped his life settle outside where they live the anonymous existence of things . . . an intention, a thought, a project can detach itself from the personal subject and become visible outside . . . his body, in the midst of what he has constructed (like a) thought that dwells outside conjuring in the world the background unknown to me."
>
> (Merleau-Ponty, 1945)

Thinking in these terms implies, on the one hand, that non-differentiated areas of the psyche (which, I repeat, should not be confused with de-differentiated areas, which are already defensive processes against poorly established differentiations) play throughout life an essential role in "revitalizing" processes of differentiation and, on the other hand, that inside/outside differentiations are plural in an individual, maintaining some fluidity and mobility. I would go further: this fluidity might be a determining criterion of mental health and can vary, depending on the individuals but also on the periods and difficulties they face in life.

In this model, human psychic spaces are therefore neither "internal" nor "external": specific to each person, they are composed of an inseparable intertwining of an "imaginary" thread, felt as "my inner world", a "realistic" thread, felt as "the external world", and a "symbolic" thread that structures him/her according to the logics specific to the different psychic configurations. To some extent, this perspective is consistent with Freud's remark that the Id is for the Ego "its other outer world" (1923, p. 298). It seems to me that this viewpoint mirrors the third of the hypotheses summarized by Rudi Vermote (2013) about the link between non-differentiated (but Vermote speaks in this regard of undifferentiated) and differentiated psychic functioning: neither radically separate nor interwoven but situated in gradients of differentiation that nevertheless remain potentially all activatable and investable by switching from one to the other. In this article, Vermote

(2013) beautifully illustrates the moment of transition from self-centred, "self-directed" daydreaming to daydreaming "directed towards what surrounds us", such as the figure of

> "the successful man" described by Keats and Bion. . . . It is found in a letter from Keats to Benjamin Bailey: "If a sparrow comes to my window, I take part in its existence and peck at the gravel".
>
> (Vermote, 2013, p. 28)

Loewald (1949) proposes a metapsychological viewpoint close to the one developed here. He starts from the hypothesis of a first non-differentiation between the baby and its environment, to assume, like Winnicott but above all, from an anthropological perspective, like Gilbert Simondon (see previously), that "the psychological constitution of the Ego and of the external world go hand in hand" (Loewald, 1949, p. 351) and that in the beginning "reality is not external but rather contained within the pre-Ego of primary narcissism" (p. 354).

He quotes the passage of *The Discontent in Culture* where Freud, discussing Rolland's "oceanic" feeling, mentions the conservation of a primary Ego – of which representative contents "would precisely be those of a lack of borders and those of a link with the Whole" – juxtaposing itself with the Ego of maturity "of which the borders are tighter and clearer" (Freud, 1930, p. 254). Loewald stresses that the synthesis functions of the Ego struggle not against the perception of reality but against the loss of reality resulting from two opposite movements: the loss of the link between the Ego and its objects, due to a gap that has become too big because of increasingly complex differentiations of the investment of the latter, and to a loss of the borders of the Ego. So, "facing a threat to the existing integration Ego-reality, the Ego and the reality find themselves reintegrated at a different level" (1949, p. 362). Referring to the loss of reality in schizophrenia, Loewald points out that it does not result initially from a withdrawal by the subject but from a regressive modification of the borders between the Ego and its reality.

Loewald's article clearly shows that the "external reality" is a construct that satisfies the individual's need to differentiate himself from an "outside" in order to feel that he exists while maintaining a close link with this outside which is, "in reality", a part of the Self. He shows that Ego and reality are "in reality" not dissociable, any change in their integration resulting in joint changes. Consequently, "omnipotence is not something that the Ego experiences only within himself; reality is also omnipotent (whether it is so for the 'objective' observer or not) and against this, the Ego can experience himself as completely impotent" (p. 364).

Loewald proposes a model of individual psychic development and functioning very close to the one I have worked out:

> I mentioned earlier that Freud had raised the issue of psychological survival of more primitive stages alongside the later stages of Ego development, an issue which he said had only briefly been touched upon. If we closely observe people, we can see that it is not only a question of the survival of earlier stages of Ego-reality integration, but that people move from one stage of integration to another, almost continuously, day by day, at different periods of their lives, according to moods and situations. Actually, it seems that more people are alive (not necessarily more "stable" however), more their range of Ego-reality levels extends. It is possible that the so-called fully developed Ego, the Ego that would have reached its full maturity, would not be the one that would have settled at the highest or most advanced stage of development, leaving other stages behind, but rather the one that integrates its reality so that the more primitive and deeper stages of Ego-reality integration remain alive as dynamic sources of a higher organization.
>
> (p. 365)

A similar opinion is also found in Bollas (2007):

> On the one hand, he [Freud] knew that an unconscious part of the person was primitive; that it included the history of the beginnings of the species, infantile sexual fantasies and was also the source of the drives. On the other hand, dream work revealed a particularly sophisticated way of thinking. How can the primitive unconscious and the sophisticated unconscious be conciliated? In fact, the contradiction disappears if we simply understand that, at the beginning, the form and the contents (i.e. the process and its productions) of the infant's unconscious are both primitive.
>
> With time, though, the Ego of the Self becomes more complex. Not that the primitive elements of the unconscious – drives, infantile fantasies, envy, greed, etc. – cease to exist, but the unconscious processing of these contents is simply becoming more subtle. Indeed, from the beginning of life, the Self works on what is primitive by dreaming, transforming visceral needs ("urges") into images.
>
> (p. 100)

Roussillon (2008a), in a chapter entitled "The Transitional Construction of 'External Reality'", indicates that Freud, after 1920, sees perception no longer as a raw "datum" of experience, but "as a process that is organized from the soma, and which, before reaching consciousness, must 'pass through' the entire psychic apparatus and must therefore be 'transformed' and organized by all the psychic systems that it goes through" (p. 234). Thus, the "reality" that has been built up in this way is experienced as "external" by the conscious Ego that obliterates the path followed by the perception going from its investment by the drive to its transformation by the more or less differentiated systems that it passes through. The "understanding" of reality will therefore vary according to the path followed by the "perceptual representation". Roussillon describes the four stages of this construction of reality: a process of decomposition and then recomposition of perception (Varela, 1993); drive investment of the Percept (which he relates to Freud's "attribution judgment") and experience of perceptive pleasure, as the source of auto-eroticisms; destruction of the object in fantasy and simultaneous survival of the object in perception, the main process to access the depressive position described by Winnicott as *the use of the object* (1971) which, as Delaunoy (1989) already pointed out, builds "external" reality for the subject; and, fourth, the constitution of the third party absent from the perception but present as "Other" of the object and represented as such:

> The permanence of the object and the investment of the object, essential components of the construction of the concept of external reality, therefore depends on the overlapping of the internal representation of the object and the potential perception of the object by a third party.
>
> (Roussillon, 2008a, p. 247)

This phase, which goes hand in hand with the organization of the fantasy of the "primal scene", is that of the *ternary organization of the concept of reality* which opens access to the recognition and sharing of a common "external" reality.

Another important point in Roussillon's development of this theme lies in the hypothesis of a "derivation of the psychic envelopes from perceptive sensoriality" (2008a, p. 243): each of the sensory modalities would build up, on the basis of specific auto-eroticisms that it generates, a set of psychic envelopes characterized by a type of relationship to the object and its "reality", tasted, felt, heard, touched, seen, spoken, linked by transmodal perceptions.

The Disseminated Self and the different psychic envelopes imply, however, one or more stabilizing functions, which I conceive, on the one hand, as dynamic stability that lies in the fluidity of the circulation between different levels of differentiation, ensured by the transitional functioning that gives shape to non-differentiated elements but, on the other hand, as static stability, due to the specificities of the self-organization of the Freudian

Ego, based on a differentiation inside-outside corresponding to the limits of the somatic body, the inside being experienced on the conscious and preconscious level as I-subject. The particularity of this self-organization would be to set up a reflexivity – that is, a symbolization of the symbolization processes themselves – particularly in relation to the "cognitive" dimensions of language. Furthermore, the configuration of the Ego, as the depositary of one of the essential functions for the stability of the Disseminated Self, proves fully functional only insofar as it is completed and counterbalanced by sufficient fluidity of the passages towards other configurations implementing other modalities of differentiation and envelopes, allowing at the same time the widest possible understanding of the totality of the individual psychic space (whose limits remain nevertheless unattainable and unknowable) while preserving a sufficient coherence and continuity of the feeling of individual identity based on the reflexive function.

I do not think, therefore, that the different primary, secondary and, as I propose, tertiary symbolizations (symbolizations of man's relationship to his technical objects) are specific to the "Ego": on the contrary, they occur in the entire psychic field, but the functionings of the Ego would have the particularity of organizing its activation and inscription in such a way as to ensure a "basic" stability to the complexity of the psyche in line with the development of the language functions. Therefore, there would be, in this approach, three levels of organization of the heterogeneity of the "psychic raw material": the level of symbolizations, which make it possible to give forms to the primary psychosomatic chaos; the level of psychic configurations, which organizes these forms in such a way so as to ensure for them an internal coherence, generating psychic envelopes and sufficiently varied inside/outside differentiations and acknowledging the existence of different types of understanding, conscious and unconscious, of oneself, of other humans and of the world; and, finally, the level of the functioning of the Ego, which ensures a sufficient stabilization of the first two by the predominance of an inside/outside differentiation that is consistent with the physical limits of the somatic body. And, to complete this organization, the vitality of non-differentiation zones supporting transitional functioning to maintain circulation between the different psychic configurations by limiting de-realization feelings and catastrophic anxiety.

It seems that this model is not unrelated to the conceptions developed by the Chilean psychoanalyst Ignacio Matte Blanco (1998–1995) when working with schizophrenic patients (Delaunoy, 2010). He defines two principles – generalization and symmetry – governing unconscious functioning. The principle of generalization states that any individual element must be considered a subset of a larger whole, and so on *ad infinitum*. The principle of symmetry treats the opposite terms of an asymmetrical relationship as if they were identical and the relationship as if it were symmetrical. So, the Unconscious is considered an infinite set of infinite sets, situated in a number of dimensions exceeding the Euclidean space and chronological temporality. On the contrary, conscious thinking is characterized by increasingly elaborate differentiations that take place in a four-dimensional space, which implies that what can be represented at the conscious level corresponds to a reduction of much larger unconscious entities.

Such a topical and dynamic contextualization opens up new fields for psychoanalysis, building on its previous achievements but placing them in a broader perspective and opening up the possibility of metapsychological developments that may make it possible to extend the efficiency of psychoanalysis to psychotic functioning and identity issues but also to new kinds of suffering resulting from the effect of social changes on the individual psychic organization itself.

In particular, the role of projection needs to be reconsidered when inside/ outside differentiations are plural: what is perceived as "external" according to a level of differentiation can be perceived as "internal" when the Self investment is placed on a different inside/outside differentiation; this is reflected, for example, by the way in which social networks lead to a suspension of the distinction between intimacy and "extimacy" (Gozlan, 2016) or by the reduction of hallucinatory phenomena observed among schizophrenic patients through the use of avatars in specific video games (Craig et al., 2015).

The distinctions between pathological splitting and functional splitting (Bayle, 2012) can also be considered not only in relation to the levels of contradictions between the split parts but also in terms of topical positions in which the substitutes are more or less blocked. This steers interpretative work less towards a confrontation of apparently contradictory positions than towards what prevents from locating them at different and potentially complementary levels of thought and being.

Equally, the issue of the relationship between destructiveness and creativity is no longer univocal but varies according to the psychic envelope within which it is considered: what appears as destructiveness in an organized envelope, for instance, according to an oedipal configuration, can be seen as bearing a potential for creativity in an envelope of lower differentiation between the self and the environment, which in turn will also considerably modify the psychic working through.

It is therefore potentially the whole metapsychological construct that can be revisited in this "polytopic" perspective, since the dynamic and economic aspects are modified according to the topical levels where they apply. When conflictual dynamics are not resolved by the production of new connections or new symbolizations, they produce an accumulation of tensions that reach levels that generate anxiety, the types of anxiety differing according to the differentiation inside/outside of each configuration. This saturation reflects the decisive importance of the economic perspective in the processes of configuration differentiation and in the transition from one configuration to another, inasmuch as the saturation of one configuration exerts an intense pressure that prompts investment – or even emergence – of another configuration. In my opinion, this is the way to understand Bion's point in view as stated in *Transformations*: "The psycho-analytic conception of cure should include the idea of a transformation whereby an element is saturated and thereby made ready for further saturation" (1965, p. 153).

It therefore appears that this field of research has already been touched upon by Winnicott and Bion, in particular, but also by other psychoanalysts whom I have "met" when reading them, although this topic dimension of their theories was not received as a "chosen fact", to quote the concept used by Bion, allowing the positing of a new paradigm for metapsychology.

As outlined in the first part of this book, the topic of the Disseminated Self can also give psychoanalysts adequate theoretical tools to help identify and make intelligible, through collaborations with other fields of knowledge, the challenges of social evolution, in particular the ongoing ecosystem disaster, in order to give back to Mankind an individual and collective "power of acting" that is more creative and less self-destructive. Perhaps this might be the object of a psychoanalytical *Weltanschauung*?

5 Vertexes, ambiguity and transitional dynamics

The lines of thought on which I base the formulation of the topical perspective of the Disseminated Self are in keeping with a current of thought of authors described as "post-Kleinian", Bion and Bleger. However, I think it is more interesting to consider the innovative contributions of these two authors as offering bridges between different psychoanalytical theories, those of Klein, where splitting lies at the base of psychic functioning, and those of other authors, especially Winnicott, but also French psychoanalysts who position themselves in a divergent way compared to the dominant currents of psychoanalytic societies, such as Anzieu, Houzel, Kaës and, to some extent, Roussillon.

Bion: vertexes, selected facts, constant conjunctions, caesurae

What I mean by "psychic configurations" is related to what Bion conceives as "models" from which experience is organized and represented in order to stabilize itself as a sense of reality. These "models" lead to "changes of perspectives" that he identifies in his early work on groups (Bion, 1961) and that he calls vertexes in his book *Transformations* (1965). When treating the psychotic functioning of some patients (1967), he observes changes in the spatial but also in the sensory vertexes, which he hypothesized to be "counterparts", on a psychic level, of somatic and temporal functioning. Bion theorizes the emergence of these "models" from the concept of *chosen facts* (borrowed from the mathematician Raymond Poincaré): it develops in the analyst's mind, "an 'evolution', namely, the coming together, by a sudden precipitating intuition, of a mass of apparently unrelated incoherent phenomena which are thereby given coherence and meaning not previously possessed (1967, p. 127).

> Within the material brought by the patient, a configuration emerges, a bit like a kaleidoscope, which seems to relate not only to the current

situation, but to many other situations which until then did not seem to have any connection between each other and that this configuration was not intended to connect.

(pp. 144–5)

Commenting on this passage, Correale (2006, p. 72) points out that "from a collection of perceptual and emotional facts, initially scattered and fragmented, the psyche distinguishes an organizing factor, the chosen fact, that will act as a constant conjunction allowing an integrated representation of this set".

It seems very important to me to take into consideration Bion's vision of a "polytopic" nature of the psyche in order to avoid the risk of a reification of the psychic reality but also of a reductive vision of the psychic functions viewed through the prism of theories that "split" them excessively, such as a too-radical distinction between psychotic and non-psychotic parts of the personality.

The descriptive approach to configurations as I envision them in this book can be linked to Bion's work on transformations. If configurations imply a topical perspective, dynamic and economic dimensions (especially the notion of saturation) as well as genetic dimensions (the development perspective) are also important in the model.

Bion uses the word "configuration" quite frequently, but to my knowledge, authors who have studied his work in depth have not paid particular attention to it. This is probably because Bion used the term descriptively, not as a concept. In his book *Transformations* (without having made an exhaustive survey of its occurrence), "configuration" is used to designate, in a descriptive manner, for example, "the configuration of the case" (1965, p. 96) and "a configuration of lines" (p. 104); however, Bion's use of it at the very end of *Transformations* seems to me to be close to my proposal:

The configuration which can be recognized as common to all development processes whether religious, aesthetic, scientic or psycho-analytical is a progression from the "void and formless infinite" to a saturated formulation which is finite and associated with number, e.g. "three" or geometric, e.g. the triangle, point, line or circle.

(p. 170)

Here, configuration seems to be part of a general trend, embodied in different "constant conjunctions".

A configuration, as I understand it, is nothing more than a structure which organizes the experience, implying a differentiation inside/outside that is its own. This structure provides the organizational elements that characterize the configuration that is being considered. It is therefore not very different from Bion's concept of "constant conjunction": "Confronted with the unknown, 'the void and formless infinite', the personality of whatever age fills the void (saturates the element), provides a form (names and binds a constant conjunction) and gives boundaries to the infinite (number and position)" (p. 171).

Vermote situates the "caesura" in Bion's work between Chapters 10 and 11 of *Transformations* (Vermote, 2019, p. 123). It is indeed in the last part of the book that an in-depth revision of the models previously developed by Bion begins, concerning the O transformations. Is part of this perspective (pp. 147–8) the unknowable nature of the absolute reality of "any object" represented by "O"; the "real self" (p. 148), something like a vanishing point in Bion's question: "Is it possible through psycho-analysis interpretation to effect a transition from knowing the phenomena of the real self to being the real self?" (1965, p. 148); "the Godhead" (p. 148), the "religious" way of naming the "ultimate object", which is never entirely accessible but constitutes this "real self" towards which all psychoanalytical work is directed according to Bion; "formless infinite" (p. 150), on which the connection processes "conquer" defined spaces and forms for the individual psyche, for example, the work of symbolization, differentiation and representation.

A transformation can only take place if the analyst and the patient have managed to "dwell" in the same configuration within the analytical field. Bion points out that "the analytical situation requires a greater depth of field than can be provided by a Euclidean model" (p. 114). From there on, I distinguish two categories of transformations: those that are evolutions within the same configuration and those that make a configuration "jump", resulting in a transition of the analytical couple into a space characterized by a different psychic envelope. These two categories only partially coincide with Bion's categories "rigid transformations" ("transfer of certain characteristics from one situation to another") and "projective transformations" (from one medium to another") (cf. p. 97), insofar as constant conjunctions tend to be more difficult to locate once a jump in configuration has taken place.

In one of his last articles (1975), Bion introduced the concept of caesura. It opens up the possibility of various understandings which is, in my opinion, a way of confronting the reader precisely with the very experience of caesura. Bion speaks of "non-pathological splitting" on the part of the analyst when the latter seeks to discern, within the patient's "whole" personality, different vertexes. "What makes the venture of analysis difficult", writes Bion,

> is that one constantly changing personality talks to another. But the personality does not seem to develop as it would as it were a piece of

elastic being stretched out. It is as if it were something like an onion does. This point adds importance to the factor of caesura, the need to penetrate what is recognized as a dramatic event like birth, or a possibility of success, or a breakdown . . . we are dealing with a series of skins which have been epidermis or conscient, but are now "free associations".

(p. 47)

Bion then wonders how to get through the different types of caesura encountered. He does not give a direct answer to this question but makes a somewhat cryptic allusion to "transitory thoughts": "Artists, musicians, scientists, discoverers", he writes, are people particularly prone to developing this type of thought, and "It is in the course of transit, in the course of changing from one position to another, that these people seem to be the most vulnerable – as, for example, during adolescence or latency" (p. 53).

Furthermore, the analyst proceeds by "transive statement on the way to an interpretation" (p. 50). It seems to me that this category of "transitory" thoughts referred to by Bion falls within the field of transitional phenomena described by Winnicott.

José Bleger: ambiguity and syncretic organization

Bleger, who described himself as Kleinian, is, however, close to Winnicott in his view of a first stage of development of the psyche, prior to the schizo-paranoid position described by Klein, which he calls "ambiguity", or in other places "syncretic organization", in reference to Wallon's work from which he drew inspiration. It is a primitive non-differentiated organization, characterized, he writes, by "the co-existence of multiple, non-integrated nuclei of ambiguity . . . each nucleus of this 'granular' Ego is itself defined by a lack of discrimination between Ego and non-Ego" (1967, p. 208).

Leopoldo Bleger (2017, p. 169) notes that, for José Bleger, "in the agglutinated nucleus, there is no object relationship between the objects and the nuclei of the Ego". This description seems very close to Winnicott's description of states of non-integration where there is no discrimination between the baby and his environment. José Bleger also points out that ambiguity is marked by an omnipotence that is not an omnipotent control of reality: "it is a way of structuring and experiencing the world, not of avoiding it. It is a specific organization of the Ego-world" (1967, p. 228).

Omnipotence (in the ambiguous personality) does not result from a negation of reality . . . a negation of reality does not exist where undifferentiation has been preserved . . . ambiguity is not, in essence, a deficit of identity: it is another identity and another sense of reality.

(p. 229)

It should be emphasized that, in Bleger's description, this phase of ambiguity is a normal stage of development.

On the other hand, it is the persistence of this ambiguous structure that leads to a specific pathological organization, which Bleger calls "symbiosis". This is defined by the transformation of ambiguous nuclei into what he terms "agglutinated nuclei", perhaps due to a movement of defensive regression (Bleger is not very clear about this transformation), a bit like the "disintegration", described by Winnicott in psychosis being a form of pathological regression to something similar, but reinvested in a defensive mode underpinned by catastrophic anxieties, to primitive states of non-integration. Let us note once again the considerable contribution of Winnicott's terminology, which systematically makes it possible to distinguish between non-differentiation and "de-differentiation", non-integration and disintegration, to qualify on the one hand that which relates to the not-yet-happened, the unformed potential from which something can be shaped, and on the other hand defensive regression to a "de-differentiation" that freezes a fortress of confusion as a shield against an intolerable differentiation that threatens the continuity of the sense of existence.

The syncretic or ambiguous state is characterized by a non-discrimination between the primitive outlines of the self and the non-self that is not accompanied by a sense of confusion. Confusion occurs only when discrimination, which has begun to be established, is secondarily lost in a defensive regressive movement (Bleger, 1967, p. 47). Leopoldo Bleger (2017, p. 172) states that

ambiguity is often confused with confusion, but the latter corresponds to the feeling when facing ambiguity, in countertransference. One must distinguish the ambiguity of the subject from the effect it produces on the person with whom he or she is talking.

So, ambiguity, as a primary non-differentiation, falls into the category of the unformed as used by Winnicott. It can be seen as a source and a reserve of creativity for the psyche.

Symbiosis is constituted, in José Bleger's theory, as a defensive formation against ambiguity, when ambiguous nuclei are rigidly transformed into agglutinated nuclei. For Bleger, such a transformation seems inevitable, underpinning everyone's psychotic areas of functioning. It's all about either keeping zones of functional ambiguity or, on the contrary, their more or less important transformation into symbiotic functioning underpinned by a specific projective defence, "agglutinated", in which the internal object in the process of differentiation finds itself crumbled and projected onto the "depository" in order to be, in a second stage, reincorporated as an agglutinated nucleus. In fact, Bleger basically describes an early failure of projective identification, which can be explained by a failure of the transformative function of "maternal reverie" (Bion) or "primary maternal concern" (Winnicott).

It is important to point out, however, that Bleger explicitly examines the possibility of mobilizing the agglutinated nuclei, which could be transformed by a process he describes as "metamorphosis" (Bleger, 1967, p. 230). The term "metamorphosis" suggests an identification process characteristic of the animic ontology described by the anthropologist Descola (2005).

Leopoldo Bleger (2017) points out, referring to the concept of syncretism developed by José Bleger (1973), that

> one of the issues at stake is to rethink the question of narcissism, to reformulate it in terms of syncytial structure. Primary narcissism assumes an isolated subject that will connect and gradually develop relationships with others and the outside world, whereas the syncytial structure implies that the subject must gradually differentiate himself during development, changing his relationship with the outside world.
>
> (Bleger, 2017, pp. 172–3)

This remark is important because it enables us to distinguish a "syncytial" narcissism, in which the libidinal investment focuses on the primitive unit "self-environment", from Freud's "primary narcissism", which "assumes an isolated subject who will connect and gradually relate to others and the outside world" (pp. 172–3). It seems to me particularly important to maintain this distinction between an area of the psyche remaining in the register of non-differentiation, and an area organized under the aegis of de-differentiation, that underlies psychotic functioning.

For instance, it also leads us to put into perspective Bleger's hypotheses on immobilization of syncretic aspects of personality by and within the framework: this immobilization concerns both de-differentiated parts but also a potential for non-differentiation, which accounts for the possibilities of non-catastrophic changes in organizations, societies and cultures.

Symbiosis is a process of projective cross-identifications between the depositor and the depositary (Bleger takes up Pichon-Rivière's distinction between the depositor, the deposited and the depositary and differentiates the projection that remains without effect on the depositary from the one where the depositary "acts" the role corresponding to the deposited), resulting in interweaving roles. The challenge for the analyst in handling the treatment is to play his role as depositary without merging with the deposited, that is, without losing his personality and identity (which requires an analysis of projective counter-identification) (1967, p. 114): "the crucial technique moment is the introduction of a splitting between the analyst and the deposited (projected) inside him. We must separate the role of psychoanalyst, that we must assume, from that of depositary, that we must play" (p. 115): the repetition of these moments leads to the fragmentation of the agglutinated nucleus.

From a technical viewpoint, Bleger distinguishes between split interpretations (splitting between the psychoanalyst and what is projected in him), which provoke a re-introjection, or those without splitting (not differentiating the analyst from what is projected into him), which establish a connection between inside and outside of the patient (p. 118), the two complementing each other, but the latter must in general precede the former (p. 119).

Bleger's considerations show up the delicate transitional position of "opener" that the analyst must manage to assume during the treatment of pathologies where the mental functioning of the patient is stuck in some rigid psychic configurations that are not easily mobilized because they are very defensive. In these situations, the splitting on the part of the analyst is at the same time what allows the analysis to take place and what threatens to destroy the analytical process. As a prerequisite for mobilizing this splitting, Bleger proposes relying on the distinction made by Bion between "splitting" and dissociation, which he relates to the one established by Bleuler between "Zerspaltung", "irregular fragmentation and disorganized scattering of the agglutinated object", and "Spaltung", "dissociation that separates already distinct parts" (p. 50): the first one would be specific to the glischro-caryque position, separating the Ego from the agglutinated object and undertaking to fragment the latter in order to transform it. Bleger defines the function of discriminating (synonymous for him with splitting and its loss with fusion, p. 111) as what allows the schizoid position to arise from the agglutinated nuclei.

Bleger's works enable us to picture the dramatic aspect of the dependence that characterizes the symbiotic relationship in its function of immobilization and control of the agglutinated nuclei and the intensity of suffering triggered by its endangerment:

> The loss of immobilization and control of the agglutinated object . . . is massive, with delirious episodes, paroxysmal and causes or threatens to cause total and immediate annihilation of the subject's Ego; this mobilization is accompanied by catastrophic . . . anxiety. . . . The defensive

techniques that operate when confronted with the agglutinated object are the most primitive and they too appear violently . . . dissociation, projection and immobilization.

(p. 48)

In the same vein, Meltzer (2006, p. 55) points out that "Bion believed that the processes that generate the metaphors and symbols necessary to understand dreams and dream thoughts are potentially painful processes, equivalent to what Melanie Klein described as the transition from the schizo-paranoid to the depressive position".

The changes of vertexes, and/or the operation of establishing pathways between different vertexes, entails adjustments of the therapeutic relationship and/or of the setting in order to maintain the patient's capacity to tolerate a certain amount of psychic pain, keeping it within limits that do not excessively threaten the feeling of sufficient coherence of the Self.

When the level of pain is too intense, or the threat too strong, these changes are prevented. In these instances, the processes of symbolization of experience can be reversed, producing beta elements. Equally, new ideas can give rise to "catastrophic anxieties", because, writes Meltzer (2006),

a new idea compels the individual to . . . momentarily dismantle the global structure of his inner world, in order to be able to rebuild it later integrating the new idea; during this moment of chaos, the delirious system will appear to the individual in its most seductive form.

(p. 57)

Fortunately, in less severe pathologies, or when the therapeutic devices are specifically adapted to major pathologies, these changes are also associated with a sense of discovery, clarification and easing, on which Correale (2006) insists.

6 From the transitional space to the network of transitional phenomena

These translations from one psychic space to another, which characterize our human existence, take place with more or less fluidity that proves to be crucial for our mental health and our ability to adapt to the unavoidability of our dissemination, increased by social transformations. This fluidity depends on the availability of the non-differentiated parts of the psyche, which finds its expression in the quality of our transitional functioning. Let us note in this respect that Winnicott (1951) considered the process of differentiating and connecting internal and external realities an ongoing task.

If one accepts the idea of a plurality of psychic spaces and envelopes and therefore also of a plurality of configurations and differentiations inside/outside, between which transitions are constantly taking place, throughout day and night psychic life, one comes to consider the "transitional" the set of processes that are solicited to make these continuous transitions possible while avoiding catastrophic anxieties about container loss. The "transitional" is no longer considered a space in itself, intermediate, situated for each individual between a stable and defined inside and outside, but a network of phenomena of transitional nature, providing an interstitial function between a plurality of differentiations inside/outside specific to each individual-environment complex. The transitions between these different levels – from one configuration to another – seek transitional functionings, which can be unsuccessful. The relationships between these multiple envelopes (involving heterogeneous temporal-spatial ranks), their areas of weakness, flexibility and rigidity, define for Guillaumin (1987) the topic and functional state of the system.

I wonder to what extent the PS/D oscillation, which Bion describes in *The Sources of Experience* (1962) as an essential driving force for the organization of the psyche, would not also bring into play phenomena of a transitional nature. Indeed, it seems to me to be paradigmatic of what I conceive as continuous passages from one psychic configuration to another.

Does the perspective of the O transformations, nearing a "formless infinite", represent differently the Winnicottian formless and transitional phenomena, of which the transitions from waking to sleep and, during sleep, from dreaming activity to dream formation, provide paradigmatic examples? From my point of view, the advantage Winnicott's transitional version has over Bion's "becoming O" is that it avoids the mystical connotation and the impression that this tendency towards "O" would be a kind of ecstasy reserved for a few particularly inspired Bionian psychoanalysts. In *Transformations*, Bion implicitly dismissed the question of a link between transitional phenomena and "tending towards O", pointing out that "the sense of inside and outside, internal and external objects, introjection and projection, container and contained, all are associated with K" (1965, p. 151). I think it is relatively acceptable to postulate an equivalence between Winnicott's transitional processes and Bion's "becoming O".

Switching from one configuration to another, or more precisely switching from the investment of one configuration to the investment of another configuration, presupposes that the "form" of the first configuration is temporarily disinvested, abandoned, that the subject "disregards" it, which leads him to pass through a "formless" time that is necessary to allow him to find another way to form the experience, another configuration, which is expected to be more appropriate for what is at stake in his psychic state of the moment.

Therefore, the formless, the un-differentiated, the "O" of Bion, constitutes an essential element of any mental functioning; the fact that this psychic material becomes inaccessible or, in analytical work, that its access is repeatedly hindered by the implicit or explicit theories of the analyst, will confine the analysand's mental functioning, and the analytical couple's work, to a restricted field within which the phenomenon of repetition limits the possibilities of change or even paralyzes any significant possibility of transformation.

Thus, psychic health could be seen as dependent on the mobility of the inside/outside topic, resulting in regular passages from one "world" to another, from one psychic configuration to another; the work of the analysis must pay close attention to the emergence of these transitional phenomena that constitute an "endless" variety (to use Guillaumin's expression, 1987) of "spaces" forming a transitional network. The elaboration of what hinders the functioning of these passages, resulting in paralysis of transitionality and traumatic stalemates of symbolization, is at the core of psychoanalytic work. This is very evident for the psychotic zones, where a defensive stiffening invalidates the mobility of the psychic configurations, allowing little leeway for managing inside/outside limits. These defences reduce the risk of disrupting the feeling of being but result in an impoverishment of the psychic functioning, leaving a lot of space for the destructive aspects of the repetition compulsion. But this work on psychic configurations can be found, if one pays attention to it, in any psychoanalytical treatment, placing the conditions for a possibility to mobilize the patient's and the analyst's psychic envelopes in the foreground of the transformative potential of the field/setting/system/process.

It seems to me to be closely related to the role of playing, as Winnicott defines it, and of which René Roussillon forcefully highlighted the metapsychological, developmental and therapeutic dimensions. In *"Les jeux du cadre"* (1995), the seventh chapter of a book that outlines the elements of a general theory of psychoanalytical features, Roussillon considers playing as an analyzer of the different modalities of symbolization and its stalemates. He describes various typical types of play that "interlock" with one another: "each elaborative loop forms a setting, a background, for a new and more complex game, which will support the next one" (Roussillon, 1995, p. 189). This model allows a more accurate conceptualization of the analyst's levels of intervention. It is particularly important with patients, or at traumatic moments in some patients' treatments, when what is at stake is the ability to play itself. Taking up these developments in *Logiques et archéologiques du cadre psychanalytique* (1995), Roussillon distinguishes three main categories of games: intersubjective, which is experienced with another person (peek-a-boo; spatula game) and self-subjective, in which the other person is a witness (Freud's coil game, for example). Several games particularly lend themselves to the passage from intersubjective to self-subjective: construction games, mirror games. And, third, intra-subjective games: dreaming.

For Roussillon, playing "displays all the work done by the Ego, its transforming and motor processes, that it contributes to make accessible for the child" (1995, p. 187).

In the model that I propose, play occupies an essential function to enable the passage from one psychic configuration to another. I observe that Roussillon, in another chapter of the same book in 1995, differentiated three modalities experiencing reality, determining three different senses of reality: "tripolarity (making it possible) to think through the clinical complexity of the splittings of the Ego and the differential relationships of the Ego to reality" (pp. 173–4): the "Ego-reality that is there from the beginning, directly stemming from perception", opposed to the Ego-pleasure; the reality test propped by motricity and movement; and the reality of the object experienced through its survival to destructiveness. These different senses of reality come together, but their manifestation in the psychoanalytic encounter is dependent on the modalities of the setup.

To back up my hypothesis, I borrow Roussillon's idea of

> "flexible medium" moments, strong and mutative moments, which punctuate the psychoanalytical process by creating in a precarious

figure, necessarily limited in time, an a-conflictual adequacy between setting, representation setting, transference, and analysis, moments when utopia is achieved before rediscovering itself nevertheless necessarily inhabited by a new form of conflict.

(p. 206)

The utopia that Roussillon mentions seems to me hardly compatible with the Ego of the Freudian topic: it is not only transitional but also interstitial; it is this non-place that separates and connects the spaces drawn by the psychic configurations, a kind of conjunctive tissue of the topics of the Self. The movement of taking/untaking/taking back described by Roussillon is a movement of topical transposition, of transfiguration. This movement is accompanied, as he also notes, by an elated feeling of jubilation. This particular affect, which was identified by Lacan in the "assumption of the I" during the mirror stage, must be differentiated from pleasure: I would pose the hypothesis that pleasure is an experience that is developed within a given psychic space; it is an experience that is specific to one psychic configuration. On the contrary, joy would testify to the success of the passage from one psychic configuration to another, which allows a true introjection, that is, the subjective appropriation of an opening of the psychic space ("a self-discovery").

The role of interpretation – that Winnicott recommended at the end of his life be reserved for exploring what the analyst does not understand – is perhaps the most effective when it deals with what prevents passage from one psychic configuration to another: the stalemates of play between psychic configurations.

Conclusion
The Disseminated Self and the perspective of complex dynamic systems

This book clearly requires further development, on both the clinical and theoretical levels. On this last level, I think that psychoanalysis could benefit a lot from transdisciplinary approaches. This conclusive chapter opens perspectives towards this. Complex dynamic systems theories could provide an adequate frame in this direction, as shown by the two following lines of work.

The transduction of the trace

The issue of the emergence of the psyche, of its development and its extension, obviously exceeds the sole field of psychoanalysis. The counterpart of this conviction is the necessity for psychoanalysis to consider theories stemming from psychic care clinical practices in their relationship with other fields of knowledge that concern the nature of the human being. One of the problems of this counterpart lies in the difficulty of circumscribing these fields of knowledge, which could extend far beyond the so-called human sciences. One way of partially resolving the problem – congruent with the fact that it is the encounter with patients in therapeutic settings that gives legitimacy and consistency to our psychoanalytical theories – would be to start from the individual and gradually extend from this centre our field of understanding of human realities.

Jean Laplanche, through his theory of generalized seduction, proposed a model that places the unknown of sexuality at the core of the emergence of the drive in the encounter between infant and adult. In a recent article, Dominique Scarfone (2020) explores the notion of "trace", starting with Laurence Kahn's criticism of Laplanche's concept of the *enigmatic signifier*. For Scarfone, the trace cannot be seen as a positive imprint, but as "an evanescent presence . . . barely conceivable and even less detectable as such". The problem is that of the use in the field of representations of a concept that refers to a "thing" that is at the same time original, unrepresentable and nevertheless essential to think through the "psychic".

Scarfone refers to the theory of autopoietic living systems developed by Varela and Maturana: "A system", he writes,

> is something that auto-organises itself by means of an "operational fence" – a semi-permeable barrier through which circulation is possible under certain conditions, but which guarantees the permanence of the system's internal laws against what is constituted as an environment.
>
> (Scarfone, 2020, p. 367)

The establishment of an inside and an outside is therefore a determining element for the constitution of a system, and autopoiesis "is the functioning that ensures self-repair and permanent self-maintenance of the system within a dynamic relationship with its environment". From this perspective, the sociologist Niklas Luhman considers *language* (understood on a general level and so having to be distinguished from the level of the different specific languages, as Scarfone reminds us based on Saussure's work) a "non-system". Scarfone adopts this idea and looks upon language as what best ensures "a 'coupling' between the individual psychic system and the environment constituted by the socio-cultural system" (Scarfone, 2020, p. 369). On the other hand, he assimilates the trace to this "untranslatable enigma" of adult sexuality which, in Laplanche's model, contaminates the message (which therefore becomes a "compromised message") addressed to the infant and constitutes the *Sexual*, a neologism proposed by this author. Scarfone introduces the idea, which is not found as such in Laplanche's work, that this "border noise", "untranslatable", is subjected to a "transduction", a "transductive leap", that is, the "structuring propagation" (Simondon, 1989) of a signal accompanied by a transformation (Scarfone speaks of "transmutation") of its nature, allowing it to become part of the structural features of the "reception" system. It is the fact that the untranslatable adult sexuality is, as it were, intertwined with an "ordinary" message in the adult's meaningful communication with the baby or toddler that requires the transduction of this "irritating trace", this parasitic "noise". It is from this process that the enigmatic *signifiers* that are already in themselves at a representational level result. Scarfone notes that this "irritating" trace necessarily produces a topical differentiation within the psyche, which he relates to the Freudian instances; "transduction" does not occur only between the individual psyche and the "environment", co-emerging during the process of individuation (Simondon) but also between the "various systems embedded in each other (for example from ics to pcs-cs)" (Scarfone, 2020, p. 371). Scarfone posits that the Freudian "*fueros*", those untranslatable "remnants" that result from the always partial nature of the passages from one level of representation/symbolization to another, can be the object of the same "transductive" process. Therefore, it would appear from these perspectives that "transduction does not transform the trace itself; it forces the psyche to reorganize itself autopoietically, to recompose itself when faced with the upsetting effect of the trace" (Scarfone, 2020, p. 378). This model of the emergence of topical differentiations seems to me consistent with that of the configurations I have outlined in this book. However, to what extent do Scarfone's propositions concern the psyche as a whole or, in a more limited way, the field of drives that psychoanalysis traditionally focuses on?

The self as a complex dynamic system

In this respect, I will mention here the French psychologist Benoît Virole's work, who, starting off with his psychoanalytic training and practice, became interested – in the context of his work with deaf and autistic children – in cognitive sciences, then in the theories of complex systems and in René Thom's theory of disasters (Virole, 2019).

Virole aims to reduce what he identifies as the "epistemological disjunction" of psychoanalysis in relation to the general scientific movement. In an article entitled "The Crisis of Psychoanalysis" (2011), he points out "the difference between a scientific approach postulating the discontinuity of reality and the psychoanalytic approach positing the continuous nature of drives . . . [based on] . . . the maintenance of an unmeasurable energy metaphor" (p. 7). "It is therefore", he writes, "up to psychoanalysis to open up if it does not want to die or become the agent of a contemporary obscurantism" (p. 12).

Virole points out that

> the complexity of living things is far beyond reach for any theoretical system but that it is possible to achieve local sections of intelligibility within this complexity. . . . None of these sections of intelligibility can claim they cover the entire complex system of living things. Nevertheless the objects that are studied are tied together in the development of the system and belong to different levels of integration.
>
> (p. 8)

Therefore, Virole proposes to use the paradigm of complex dynamic systems. He states that "a complex system allows the articulation between a continuous variable and a discontinuous appearance" (p. 8). He therefore proposes re-examining psychoanalytical epistemology from this perspective and to do so to describe some interfaces between psychoanalysis' dynamic system and other scientific systems.

The first issue for him is to define the theoretical axes that make it possible to ensure a minimal but sufficient coherence in psychoanalysis. He suggests retaining three main points: the existence of the unconscious; the continuous character of the sexual drive (differentiated from instinct); and identification, in its objectal and narcissistic registers.

He bases the second phase on the *Theory of Psychic Attractors*; in a homonymous article, published in 2016, he introduces the idea that "psychic activity, emerging from neuronal interconnectivity, has similar properties as those of a dynamic system with constantly interacting attractors" (Virole, 2016a, p. 2). We have already encountered in this book the notion of an "attractor" with Houzel's work. Virole defines an "attractor" as

> a position of relative stability within the complex dynamic set of mental representations, emotions, and generally speaking all mental states. An attractor draws towards a position of stability the evolving paths of thoughts, beliefs, feelings, emotions and fantasies. An attractor can diverge into another type of attractor, split, merge by resonances (similarities) or be in a dynamic conflict with one or more other attractors. . . . The various mental states are the result of complex interactions between these attractors. Under certain conditions, one mental state takes over and becomes dominant until a change in the parameters controlling the system causes it to branch off into another state. This dynamic system is controlled by the development of a regulation figure, as defined by René Thom, i.e. a structure that integrates various external parameters, some of which are themselves under the control of the genome. However, the genome controls the branching out points between the attractors but not the whole system.
>
> (p. 2)

Virole then describes four attractors, roughly corresponding to the "positions" of the Kleinian and post-Kleinian school. He also hypothesizes the existence of an active system oscillating between these different attractive positions that accounts for the generative nature of creative and abstract processes, similar to the one described by Bion for the schizo-paranoid/depressive oscillation (projection/introjection). This hypothesis of psychic attractors broadly corresponds to what underlies the organization of psychic configurations. In another article published in 2016, "Topic of Complexity", Virole develops the hypothesis that the psyche "can be described by a topical arrangement, i.e. a spatial description of its constituent elements allowing the execution of its functions" (2016b, p. 1), the topic of the Self. "The self", he writes, "is the topic with the highest complexity allowing the interface of the individual with collective systems through individuation and virtualization functions (anticipatory projection of self-realization)" (p. 2).

Virole describes the Self as a holistic instance (whose global functioning goes beyond the simple juxtaposition of its constituents); its nature is autopoietic (Varela, 1995); its self-regulation is teleonomic (it merges with its of existence); its structural stability is dependent on the psychic attractors that constitute fields of regulation.

In terms of psychic individuation, Virole highlights two extreme attractive positions of narcissism, derived from Kohut's work: the grandiose Self (attempting to annihilate the social background) and the identification with an idealized parental imago generating fusion with a collective ideal.

One of the benefits of the model of the Self as a complex dynamic system developed by Virole is to propose an integrative instance where cognitive and psychoanalytical perspectives could be articulated while preserving their intrinsic logic.

So, we see that the concept of transduction, imported from an "outside" of psychoanalysis, could be viewed as another way of approaching Winnicott's transitional functions, which I see as central in the translations between psychic configurations. In the same way, Virole's concept of psychic attractors, already mentioned by Houzel, are a second core concept in the organizational model of the Disseminated Self and the psychic configurations.

Finally, clinical examples should be collected in order to illustrate and make more explicit the ideas exposed in this book. They could usefully be completed by explorations in another very important field of human experience, which both Freud and Winnicott considered to have a high value for psychoanalysis: artistic creation.

References

Ameisen J.-C. (1999), *La sculpture du vivant*, Paris, rééd. 2003.

Anzieu D. (1984), Le Groupe et l'Inconscient, Paris, Dunod, 234 p.

Anzieu D. (1985), *The Skin-Ego*, London, Routledge, 2018.

Anzieu D. (2003, dir.), *Les enveloppes psychiques*, Paris, Dunod.

Bayle G. (2012), *Clivages*, Paris, PUF.

Bion W.R. (1961), *Experiences in Groups*, London, Tavistock.

Bion W.R. (1962), *Learning from Experience*, London, Karnac.

Bion W.R. (1963), *Elements of Psychoanalysis*, London, Karnac.

Bion W.R. (1965), *Transformations*, London, Butterworth Heinemann, 2013.

Bion W.R. (1967), *Second Thoughts*, London, Butterworth Heinemann, 2013.

Bion W.R. (1975), *Two Papers: The Grid and Caesura*, London & New York, Routledge, 2018.

Bleger J. (1967), *Symbiosis and Ambiguity*, New York, Routledge, 2013.

Bleger J. (1973), Ambiguity: A Concept of Psychology and Psychopathology, in: Arieti S. (ed.) *The World Biennal of Psychiatry and Psychotherapy*, vol. 2, New York, Basic Books, pp. 453–70.

Bleger L. (2017), José Bleger: penser la psychanalyse, *Revue Française de Psychanalyse*, 81, 3: 149–83.

Bollas C. (2007), *The Freudian Moment*, Routledge, 2013.

Correale A. (2006), PS ←→ D, in: *Lire Bion*, dir. Neri C. et coll., pp. 70–5.

Craig T., Rus-Calafell M., Ward T., et al. (2015), *The Effects of an Audio Visual Assisted Therapy Aid for Refractory Auditory Hallucinations (AVATAR Therapy): Study Protocol for a Randomised Controlled Trial*, Trials, vol. 16, no 1, p. 349.

Delaunoy J. (1989), La construction de la réalité, *Revue belge de Psychanalyse*, 14: 15–27 et 15: 23–34.

Delaunoy J. (2010), Note de lecture: *Une autre pensée psychanalytique*, de Carvalho R., Ginzburg A., Lombardi R., Sachez-Cardenas M. (2006), Paris, L'Harmattan, *Revue belge de psychanalyse*, 56: 115–20.

De Micco V. (2019), Esprits Migrants, Esprits Adolescents, *Revue belge de psychanalyse*, 75: 29–47.

Descola P. (2005), *Beyond Nature and Culture*, University of Chicago Press, 2013.

Freud S. (1895), *Project for a Scientific Psychology*, in Strachey, J. (1966). The Standard Edition of the Complete Psychological Works of Sigmund Freud, Volume I

(1886–1899): Pre-Psycho-Analytic Publications and Unpublished Drafts, 1–411. The Hogarth Press and the Institute of Psychoanalysis, London.

Freud S. (1913), *Totem and Taboo*, in Strachey, J. (1955), The Standard Edition of the Complete Psychological Works of Sigmund Freud, Volume XIII (1913–1914): Totem and Taboo and Other Works, 1–255. The Hogarth Press and the Institute of Psycho-analysis, London.

Freud S. (1915), *A Metapsychological Supplement to the Theory of Dreams*, Standard Edition, vol. 14, Strachey J., 1957.

Freud S. (1923), *The Ego and the Id*, in: Strachey, J. (1961). The Standard Edition of the Complete Psychological Works of Sigmund Freud, Volume XIX (1923–1925), 1–308. The Hogarth Press and the Institute of Psychoanalysis, London.

Freud S. (1930), *Civilization and Its Discontents*, in: Strachey, J. (1961). The Standard Edition of the Complete Psychological Works of Sigmund Freud, Volume XXI (1927–1931): The Future of an Illusion, Civilization and its Discontents, and Other Works, 1–273. The Hogarth Press and the Institute of Psycho-analysis, London.

Freud S. (1933), *New Introductory Lectures on Psycho-Analysis*, in: Strachey, J. (1964). The Standard Edition of the Complete Psychological Works of Sigmund Freud, Volume XXII (1932–1936): New Introductory Lectures on Psycho-Analysis and Other Works, 1–267. The Hogarth Press and the Institute of Psycho-analysis, London.

Freud S. (1939), *Moses and Monotheism*, in: Strachey, J. (1964). The Standard Edition of the Complete Psychological Works of Sigmund Freud, Volume XXIII (1937–1939): Moses and Monotheism, An Outline of Psycho-Analysis and Other Works, 1–312. The Hogarth Press and the Institute of Psychoanalysis, London.

Gozlan A. (2016), *L'adolescent face à Facebook*, Paris, In Press.

Guillaumin J. (1987), Les enveloppes psychiques du psychanalyste. Quelques hypothèses pour une application de la théorie des enveloppes psychiques à l'étude du fonctionnement du psychanalyste, in: Anzieu D. et coll, *Les enveloppes psychiques*, Paris, Dunod.

Houzel D. (1987), Le concept d'enveloppe psychique; in: Anzieu D. et coll., Les enveloppes psychiques, Paris, Dunod.

Houzel D. (2010), Le concept d'enveloppe psychique, Paris, In Press, 188 p.

JACOBY, R. (1983), The Repression of Psychoanalysis: Otto Fenichel and the Political Freudians. Chicago: University of Chicago Press.

Kaës R. (1976), *L'appareil psychique groupal*, Paris, Dunod, rééd. 2010.

Kaës R. (2009), *Les alliances inconscientes*, Paris, Dunod, rééd. 2014.

Kaës R. (2012), *Le Malêtre*, Paris; Dunod, 278 p.

Kaës R. (2015), *L'extension de la psychanalyse*, Paris, Dunod.

Kahn L. (2018), *Ce que le nazisme a fait à la psychanalyse*, Paris, Presses Universitaires de France.

Kerr P. (1994), *Berlin Noir*, New York, Penguin Random House.

Kerr P. (2017), *Prussian Blue*, Marian Woods Book/Putnam.

Leroi-Gourhan A. (1943), *L'homme et la matière*, Paris, Albin Michel, 1971.

Leroi-Gourhan A. (1945), *Milieu et techniques*, Paris, Albin Michel, 1973.

Loewald H.W. (1949), Moi et réalité, *Revue Française de Psychanalyse*, 2001/2: 349–65.

Magnenat L. (2019), Le propre de l'homme à l'âge de l'anthropocène, in: Magnenat L. (dir.), *La crise environnementale sur le divan*, Paris, In Press, pp. 145–248.

Matot J.-P. (2014), Quel patient veut être le poème ou le tableau de quelqu'un d'autre? *Revue Belge de Psychanalyse*, 64: 31–50.

Matot J-P. (2019), *L'Homme décontenancé I. De l'urgence d'étendre la psychanalyse*, Paris, L'Harmattan.

Meltzer D. (2006), Le modèle de la psyché selon Bion: notes sur la fonction alpha, inversion de la grille alpha et grille négative, in: *Lire Bion*, dir. Neri C. et coll., pp. 53–60.

Merleau-Ponty M. (1945), *Phénoménologie de la perception*, Paris, Gallimard.

Nassikas K. (2011), *Exils de langue*, Paris, Presses Universitaires de France.

Press J. (2019a), Psychanalyse et crise environnementale, in: Magnenat L., *La crise environnementale sur le divan*, Paris, In Press, pp. 261–70.

Press J. (2019b), *Expériences de l'informe*, Paris, In Press.

Rosa H. (2010), *Acceleration and Alienation: Towards a Critical Theory of Late-Modern Temporality*, Surkamp, Insel.

Roussillon R. (1995), *Logiques et archéologiques du cadre psychanalytique*, Paris, PUF.

Roussillon R. (2008a), *Le transitionnel, le sexuel et la réflexivité*, Paris, Dunod.

Roussillon R. (2008b), *Le jeu et l'entre-je(u)*, Paris, Presses Universitaires de France.

Scarfone D. (2020), Trace et transduction, in: Bombarde O., Neau F., Matha C. (dir.), *Quelques motifs de la psychanalyse*, Paris, Les Belles Lettres, pp. 365–78.

Schwartz G. (2019), *Les amnésiques*, Paris, Flammarion.

Searles H. (1960), *The Nonhuman Environment*, International University Press.

Sheffer E. (2018), *Asperger's Children: The Origins of Autism Nazi Vienna*.

Simondon G. (1958), *Du mode d'existence des objets techniques*, Paris, Aubier, 1989.

Simondon G. (2005), *L'individuation à la lumière des notions de forme et d'information*, Grenoble, Ed. Catherine Millon, 2013.

Stiegler B. (1994), *La technique et le temps I: La faute d'Epiméthée*, Paris, Galilée.

Varela F.J., Goldstein O. (1995), The Organism. A Holistic Approach to Biology Derived from Pathological Data in Man; Zone Books, New York.

Vermote R. (2013), Le mode indifférencié du fonctionnement psychique: approche intégrative et implications cliniques, *Bulletin de la Fédération européenne depsychanalyse*, 67: 19–31.

Vermote R. (2019), *Reading Bion*, London & New York, Routledge.

Virole B. (2011), *La crise de la psychanalyse*, www.benoitvirole.com/.

Virole B. (2016a), *Théorie des attracteurs psychiques*, www.benoitvirole.com/.

Virole B. (2016b), *Topique de la complexité*, www.benoitvirole.com/.

Virole B. (2019), *Catastrophes de l'Inconscient*, Pantin, Editions Baghera.

Vuillard E. (2017), *L'ordre du jour*, Arles, Actes Sud.

Winnicott D.W. (1951), Objets transitionnels et phénomènes transitionnels, in: *Through Paediatrics to Psycho-Analysis*, London, Karnak Books, 1992.

Winnicott D.W. (1952), L'angoisse associée à l'insécurité, in: *De la pédiatrie à la psychanalyse*, Paris, Payot, 1969.

Winnicott D.W. (1954), Les aspects métapsychologiques et cliniques de la régression au sein de la situation analytique, in: *De la pédiatrie à la psychanalyse*, Paris, Payot, 1969.

Winnicott D.W. (1971), Playing and Reality, New York, Routledge, 2005.

Winnicott D.W. (1989), *Lectures et portraits*, Paris, Gallimard, 1989.

Index

Printed in the United States
by Baker & Taylor Publisher Services